TAIИ

Flashpoints

The end of the Cold War unleashed a new era of international relations and accelerated the forces of globalization. Old conflicts reasserted themselves and the seeds of new threats were sown. This series examines those regions, relationships and issues that in the international arena have the potential to cause conflict between states. Each title offers a theoretically grounded analysis of the history, current complexion and likely outcome of the flashpoint to enrich our understanding of global politics, security and international relations.

Published

Taiwan: A Contested Democracy Under Threat
Jonathan Sullivan and Lev Nachman

TAIWAN

A Contested Democracy Under Threat

Jonathan Sullivan and Lev Nachman

agenda
publishing

First published in 2024 by Agenda Publishing

Agenda Publishing Limited
PO Box 185
Newcastle upon Tyne
NE20 2DH
www.agendapub.com

ISBN 978-1-78821-670-8 (hardcover)
ISBN 978-1-78821-671-5 (paperback)

British Library Cataloguing-in-Publication Data
A catalogue record for this book is available from the British Library

Typeset by JS Typesetting Ltd, Porthcawl, Mid Glamorgan
Printed and bound in the UK by CPI Group (UK) Ltd, Croydon, CR0 4YY

Contents

Preface

There has never been greater international interest in Taiwan, nor such widespread concern. This moment is long overdue. For decades, Taiwanese people have hoped that their achievements in economic transformation and democratic transition would be recognized, and that Taiwan could participate and contribute to international society on its own merits. For political reasons discussed throughout this book, that has not happened. Taiwan's desire to be seen as a respected player on the global stage has generally been frustrated. It is ironic that it took the intensification of PRC threats to alert global audiences to Taiwan's many achievements, and to inculcate feelings of solidarity for Taiwan's struggle. To meaningfully care about what happens in Taiwan, however, requires an understanding of what makes Taiwan special, why it matters and what can be done to keep Taiwan peaceful.

This book is pitched at readers who are new to Taiwan and want to learn more about it. We hope to introduce the complexities of Taiwan and "the Taiwan issue" in a clear and accessible way. We cannot speak on behalf of Taiwanese people or articulate what it means to be Taiwanese, but we can speak to the process of learning about Taiwan. Our research and experiences as academics can help connect those who want to know more about Taiwan. We anticipate that this group will include policymakers, journalists, businesspeople, students and concerned citizens around the world. Both authors have worked extensively with such stakeholders and have identified a need and appetite for this kind of publication. In this book, we aim to provide a comprehensive and balanced discussion of "where are we at?", an explanation of "how did we get here?", and informed speculation about "where are things heading?"

Taiwan

One of our main motivations for writing the book is to recentre Taiwan. In doing so, we want to provide an alternative to typical analyses that depict Taiwan as a passive object or define it solely as a site of potential conflict. As western academic specialists of Taiwanese politics who have spent much of our lives studying and living in Taiwan, we are keenly aware that Taiwan is frequently relegated to a "flashpoint" and a cause of nebulous "tensions". Often invoked as a political talking point or depicted as collateral damage under Sino-US competition, Taiwan's agency to affect its own future is often left out of the discussion. The complexities of contemporary Taiwanese politics and society are glossed over, and the desires of Taiwanese people barely warrant concern. Our priority with this book is to reframe how international observers perceive Taiwan and the complex environment in which it operates. We hope to enhance international understanding of Taiwan's own contested preferences and how its actions interact with those of China and the US.

The "Taiwan issue" – a heuristic that captures Taiwan's disputed sovereign status and awkward position between China and the United States – is complicated and in need of demystifying. Although the Taiwan issue has in recent years risen to an unprecedented level of salience among western policymakers and publics, there are many misunderstandings, misconceptions and partial perspectives. With this book, we aim to address these issues by examining the preferences, positions and behaviours of the major actors, primarily of course Taiwan itself. Unlike many western publications that gloss over it, we shall also consider the position of the People's Republic of China (PRC). Whether or not one agrees with it, it is important to understand what the PRC position is, where it comes from and what pursuit of its realization might lead to. Situating the PRC position within broader Sino-US relations, the security environment in East Asia and the role that Taiwan plays in domestic Chinese politics, the PRC position with regard to Taiwan is less inexplicable and more nuanced than unvariegated narratives about belligerent authoritarianism.

While interest in Taiwan itself has never been higher around the world, a fundamental understanding of Taiwanese politics and society lags behind. With this book, we aim to establish in an authoritative and accessible way how Taiwan got to where it is today, what Taiwanese politicians and civil society want and the obstacles they face in achieving it. This is a much more complicated story than popular stylized dichotomies like "democracy vs authoritarianism" or "independence vs unification". It is a story intimately tied to democratization, decolonialism, national identity, economic interdependence, multiculturalism and modern values – all set against an ever-present security dimension. As a top 20 global economy and tech powerhouse, a liberal democracy on the frontline of authoritarian pressure and a pivotal component in the "free and open Indo-Pacific", Taiwan's future will have an outsized impact on the direction of travel for regional peace and the global order.

Readers who are less familiar with Taiwan's story will bring many questions to this book. Is Taiwan part of China? Why is Taiwan such a controversial issue? How did Taiwan become democratic? How important is the Taiwanese tech industry? Could China and the US really go to war over Taiwan? These are all reasonable questions. Indeed, they cut directly to some of the most fundamental concerns. We shall address these and numerous other questions in this book. Getting to grips with Taiwan, which barely features in western curricula and is present in the news and political debates for a narrow set of reasons, can be intimidating. Where does one begin to learn about Taiwan with all its bewildering complexities and nuances? Our motivation for writing this book is to provide a starting point.

As exemplified in this Preface, "Taiwan" is a ubiquitous shorthand for the Republic of China (ROC). We discuss in a later chapter the complicated relationship between Taiwan and the ROC, but we will generally use "Taiwan" as a shorthand. We also use China and PRC interchangeably. When we refer to China, we mean the PRC and not the ROC.

* * *

The authors thank two anonymous referees for their extremely useful feedback at different stages of the writing process. We thank Jessica Drun, Eliana Ritts and Brian Hioe for reading different parts of the manuscript and providing comments. Thanks to Kerry Brown for raising the original idea to write this book and Alison Howson at Agenda for her editorial support. Thanks to Sarah Jeu for help with indexing and the Asia Research Institute at the University of Nottingham for funding it.

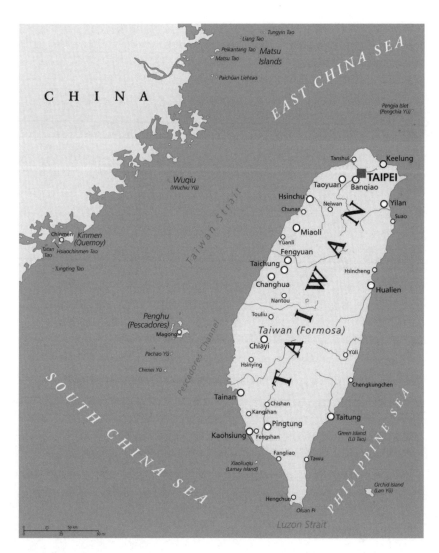

Map of Taiwan

Source: Peter Hermes Furian / Alamy Stock Photo.

1

Why Taiwan matters

There is a possibility that the next great military conflict could be fought over Taiwan. As we write this book, the likelihood of militarized conflict involving the United States and the PRC is higher than it has been for many decades. The sense of heightened "tensions" and looming conflict in the Taiwan Strait[1] has become global news broadcasts. Some readers' interest in Taiwan may have been prompted by news coverage of House of Representatives Speaker Nancy Pelosi's visit to Taipei in August 2022 and the People's Liberation Army's (PLA) live-fire military exercises that immediately followed it, or from commentators and some elected officials comparing the situation in Taiwan to Russia's invasion and war against Ukraine. But the situation in the Taiwan Strait is complex, nuanced and defies simple analogies. Peace in the Taiwan Strait is a product not just of Taiwan's own actions, but those of the PRC and the US. The preferences and actions of China and the US, and the conduct of relations between these two superpowers, have an inescapable impact on Taiwanese security, prosperity, and even Taiwan's continued existence as an autonomous polity and society. A militarized superpower conflict would be devastating for the people who call Taiwan home. It would destroy peace in the Asian region, fundamentally alter the global order and wreak havoc on the global economy. While the dire consequences of a hypothetical war are largely agreed on – including in the PRC – there is much more to the Taiwan story than conflict.

Taiwan is home to almost 24 million people, living in a hard-won liberal democratic society. Taiwan's diverse peoples – Indigenous Austronesian

---

1. The Taiwan Strait is a 180 km-wide body of water, part of the South China Sea, and separates the island of Taiwan and the Chinese Province, Fujian.

Taiwanese, transnational Hakka, immigrants from all over Southeast Asia, and different generations of Han Chinese – constitute a unique hybrid culture and society. Taiwan has been shaped by numerous colonizing powers and persevered through Kuomintang (KMT) one-party authoritarian rule to become one of the most economically vibrant and progressive societies in Asia. Taiwan's innovative tech firms, comprehensive social healthcare and marriage equality for its LGBTQ+ community are envied around the world. Remarkably, these achievements have been made against a backdrop of chronic threats to economic and national security, international marginalization, and intensifying efforts by the PRC to coerce Taiwanese people to accept a political outcome very few favour, i.e. unification.

THE TAIWAN ISSUE

Taiwan and the smaller offshore islands under its jurisdiction are claimed by the PRC. The PRC's sovereignty claim over Taiwan is emphatic – it is a core national interest that Chinese leaders credibly threaten to go to war to defend. Xi Jinping, secretary general of the Chinese Communist Party (CCP), head of the Chinese military and president of China, has stated that Taiwan must and will be "reunited" with the PRC, a country that has itself never exercised authority over Taiwan. The intimate intertwining of Chinese and Taiwanese histories, cultures and peoples is an undeniable empirical fact. Yet for many decades Taiwan and the PRC have pursued divergent and incompatible developmental paths. Taiwan has consolidated a high functioning and progressive democratic political system; whereas for all its astonishing economic and scientific achievements, and societal advances, the PRC has remained a tightly controlled authoritarian state. Taiwanese people have voiced a strong preference for retaining their autonomy and democracy. Despite economic interdependence, and cultural and linguistic commonalities, longitudinal opinion polling and other indicators show that Taiwanese people have no interest in acceding to the PRC's demands to give up Taiwan's existing autonomy. Integration into the PRC holds minimal appeal. The offer of "one country, two systems", from the PRC perspective a generous and pragmatic solution that would allow Taiwan to retain some of its current freedoms, is a political non-starter. The great majority of Taiwanese people identify with the characteristics and values embodied by Taiwan's democracy, not those of the PRC.

The PRC's sovereignty claim is a far-reaching constraint on many aspects of Taiwanese politics. For example, in terms of foreign relations, for a country to establish diplomatic relations with the PRC it must relinquish formal relations with Taiwan. The PRC's determined opposition, combined with its economic and diplomatic clout, has forced Taiwan's withdrawal from most formal modes of international participation. Taiwan is recognized by a mere handful of diplomatic allies, mostly impoverished small and micro-states. Taiwan is excluded from international organizations like the United Nations (UN), and not permitted to sit, even as an observer, in functional bodies like the World Health Organization (WHO). However, as a global powerhouse in trade, tech, medicine and other sectors, Taiwan enjoys intense unofficial and informal relations with many countries. Enjoying visa-free access to 109 countries (69 more than PRC passport holders), Taiwanese people do business, travel and study in large numbers across the world. And yet, the international community does not treat Taiwan in a way that is commensurate with its global standing as a major economy and beacon of liberal democracy in Asia. The resulting sense of indignity and marginalization is a longstanding source of frustration for Taiwanese people. The intractable contest over sovereignty, and the asymmetry inherent in a continent-sized superpower going against a much smaller island, is the context in which Taiwan operates.

Taiwan's relations with China, and its future national status, are also contested within Taiwanese society. Domestic politics in Taiwan is largely structured by divisions and social cleavages that reflect long-standing struggles over national identity. Public opinion polls show that a substantial majority of Taiwanese people now identify as Taiwanese, rather than Chinese. This has not always been the case, and it is not always clear what people mean by their declared identification. The connection between national identity and desired national status is also complicated by the PRC's threat to use force to prevent "Taiwan independence". The effect of the PRC's "independence means war" equation is that there is a substantial gap between support for Taiwanese identity and support for independence. Nevertheless, the data allow us to infer with a relatively high degree of confidence that a majority of Taiwanese people would prefer even a liminal, unrecognized and insecure Taiwan if it meant the continuation of the freedoms guaranteed by their liberal democratic political system.

The PRC demands that Taiwan relinquish its de facto independence and submit to the PRC's exercise of sovereignty. Taiwanese political parties and people largely reject this demand. This tension is at the heart of the Taiwan issue. Yet, cross-Strait relations are not solely about conflict. The cultures and societies on each side of the Taiwan Strait are deeply connected through shared cultural heritage, languages, ethnicities, and historical and contemporary migrations. Vastly different forms of government do not negate Taiwan and the PRC's reservoir of shared historical legacies and cultural affinities. The two economies are intensely connected and highly interdependent, and both are equally embedded in the global economy. Even amid the intensification of pressures and threats from the PRC, China remained Taiwan's biggest trading partner. Economic exchange over the past three decades has contributed to development and modernization on both sides of the Strait. For better and worse, relations with the PRC are fundamental to Taiwan's security and economy. This reality is reflected in one of the main areas of contestation in Taiwanese politics, namely the approach to relations with the PRC that best serves Taiwan's interests. This is sometimes crudely reduced to a question of balancing the needs of the economy (closer relations with China) and national security (more cautious relations with China). Inevitably, given Taiwan's precarious situation, economic issues are both political and geopolitical. There is no better illustration of this than Taiwan's semiconductor industry, one of the most important parts of the Taiwanese economy and a fundamental cog in the global economy, which we shall discuss in a later chapter.

BETWEEN CHINA AND THE UNITED STATES

Taiwan occupies a key strategic location in East Asia and from the founding of the PRC in 1949 it has been a site of contestation between China and the US. Notwithstanding the normalization of PRC–US relations in the 1970s and the engagement policies that facilitated China's economic transformation and assimilation into the global economy, Taiwan remained an unresolved point of contention. As China rose to become a strategic rival to the US the Taiwan issue has increased in salience, on both sides, bringing Taiwan into geostrategic competition between the US and China.

Asymmetrical power dynamics are fundamental to Taiwan's relationship with the PRC. By global standards Taiwan is wealthy and its military is modern and well resourced. Taiwan can also claim an influential diaspora and a reservoir of "soft power". Yet, the power differential between Taiwan and the PRC is substantial and growing. In the economic, military and diplomatic spheres the PRC is one of the most powerful countries in the world. This reality makes Taiwan's determination to resist the PRC's claims and preserve its autonomy remarkable – and full of risk. Resisting constant Chinese pressures and threats requires internal qualities like tenacity and perseverance. It also requires external support from like-minded supporters, albeit much of it offered tentatively and circumstantially.

The most important source of outside support for Taiwan comes from the US. Relations between the US and Taiwan are "unofficial", but this designation understates the depth and intensity of the US–Taiwan relationship. To a large extent, Taiwan's capacity to deter PRC military action depends on the US' willingness to supply appropriate weapons and on keeping the PRC guessing as to whether the US military would intervene on Taiwan's behalf in the event of conflict. Taiwan is one of the most contentious issues in Sino-US relations, and the PRC bitterly resents what it sees as American interference preventing the "sacred task" of Chinese national unification. The US and Taiwan share liberal, democratic and other values, but it suits American strategic interests for Taiwan to retain its autonomy and resist unification with the PRC. A Taiwan under PRC control would radically alter the strategic balance in the entire Western Pacific in China's favour and to the detriment of the US.

The US–China relationship has been deteriorating since the mid-2010s. Competing interests have sharpened and the complexities of managing superpower relations have intensified. The relationship is of global significance, but nowhere is it felt as keenly as in Taiwan. As US–China relations sour, the more the US has become inclined to (in some quarters, fervently and overtly) support Taiwan. While some Americans see the enhancement of the US–Taiwan alliance as beneficial to both the US and Taiwan's strategic interests, the PRC sees the US's increased support of Taiwan as a tool to use against China, which serves to further antagonize US–China relations. Others, in the US and Taiwan, worry that the US government's warming relations with Taiwan are to spite China, rather than out of genuine concern for Taiwan's well-being.

Taiwan's efforts to exercise and consolidate its autonomy while avoiding antagonizing the PRC are complicated by the growing hostility and suspicion between China and the US. Taiwan (and the US) has avoided crossing Chinese red lines, most obviously by refraining from formally declaring "Taiwan independence". From the PRC's perspective, military modernization, preparation for possible military contingencies in the Taiwan Strait and increasing hybrid-warfare activities directed at Taiwan do not negate its stated pursuit of "peaceful unification". In the face of what it sees as Taiwanese and American "provocations", China argues that it has shown great restraint in refraining from kinetic military action.

The PRC's claims over Taiwan and its behaviours in the Taiwan Strait in recent years are not simply a function of naked aggression or "authoritarian spread". They are explicable, whether or not one supports or agrees with them, and more deeply rooted than a simple "democracy versus authoritarianism" lens might suggest. That stark binary paradoxically obscures the ambiguities that for several decades facilitated a liveable equilibrium in the Taiwan Strait, but is now under threat. Trends in US and Chinese domestic politics and foreign policy suggest further difficulties ahead, circumscribing Taiwan's repertoire of available policy actions and increasing the risk of conflict. In the chapters that follow, we explain how Taiwan became enmeshed in this precarious situation and how it navigates it.

STRUCTURE OF THE BOOK

The book is organized in a way that eases readers into the study of Taiwan. From the historical antecedents of modern Taiwan it proceeds through the political contexts of the Republic of China (ROC) to contemporary issues such as the economy and security. As an introductory text, this book cannot provide exhaustive coverage of these topics, but it will provide readers new to Taiwan with essential knowledge and understanding, while pointing to some of the nuances that go beyond popular sources of information.

During the past four hundred years Taiwan has undergone numerous political transformations and experienced colonialism in several forms. Chapter 2 begins with an overview of Indigenous history and the role of Indigenous peoples in Taiwan's early settlement, before discussing Taiwan's experience of colonization by western European powers. It then shows how Taiwan became absorbed into China's sphere of influence during the Ming dynasty and was integrated into the Manchu Qing dynasty. Next, we discuss Taiwan's emergence as a Japanese "model colony" and how Japan's colonial regime established physical and institutional foundations for Taiwan's modern development. Our summary of Taiwanese history concludes with an émigré regime of authoritarian Chinese nationalism, a Cold War bastion of anti-communism under the guise of Free China, and the transformational experience of "third wave" democratization. We show how Taiwan's contemporary democratic and multicultural society embodies a "Taiwaneseness" created and infused by all of these different historical experiences and influences. Taiwan's history should not be construed solely as that of a Chinese society and cannot be fully understood without an appreciation of the multiple socio-historical layers that produce the unique Taiwanese hybridity.

The foundational position of Taiwanese citizens and political parties is that Taiwan's future should be decided by the Taiwanese people. In Chapter 3 we examine what Taiwanese people want, and by extension, what they don't want. We explain how national identity became fundamental to Taiwanese politics and society during democratization and discuss the evolution of public opinion within elites and civil society over time. This chapter begins with an overview of democratization processes and the key factors that together facilitated democratic transition. We then pivot to a close inspection of how Taiwan's democracy functions. Taiwan's political spectrum, unlike many counterpart democracies in the world, is not defined by left–right socio-economic and class issues. Instead, Taiwanese voters are more concerned about identity and the relationship with China. We detail how the political spectrum developed, and how other key political issues such as economic growth and environmental politics are (often unhelpfully) filtered through the lens of identity and sovereignty. We shall also explore how Taiwanese institutions such as exemplary voting and e-government systems facilitate democracy. Notwithstanding Taiwan's democratic achievements, challenges to the operation and quality of democracy remain. We thus note how traditional elements of political culture, incomplete democratic reforms and a sensationalist partisan media represent challenges. We finally discuss how Taiwanese elections and social movements became critical events shaping political competition and discourse.

One point of confusion for non-specialist observers of Taiwan is the relationship between Taiwan and the Republic of China (ROC), and the various related concepts attached to China–Taiwan relations ("One China", "1992 Consensus", "status quo", etc). In Chapter 4 we discuss the contested meanings and status of the ROC (internationally, in law and diplomacy) before examining how Taiwan's own relationship to the ROC has evolved from the authoritarian period through to the present day. The continued existence of the ROC is fundamental to understanding Taiwan's status and domestic political competition. For some Taiwanese, the ROC must be defended and preserved; for others it is a reminder that Taiwan's decolonization is still incomplete. For a substantial cohort of pragmatic Taiwanese citizens, the ROC is tolerated as an expedient framework in which cultural localization can proceed without claiming the formal "independence" that would ignite a cross-Strait military conflict. However, complications have emerged in the form of conceptual nuances like "the ROC vs the ROC-on-Taiwan", "ROC independence vs Taiwan independence", and the PRC's own explicit denial of the ROC's existence, despite its insistence on the "1992 Consensus" of "One China, respective interpretations". Providing the veneer of One China to Taiwanese autonomy, the ROC remains a central and keenly contested construct in cross-Strait relations.

The PRC claims sovereignty over Taiwan and is highly motivated to end the current state of separation. The PRC's formal aim is to achieve "peaceful reunification", while reserving the right to use force to prevent "Taiwan independence", and engaging in various coercive behaviours. In Chapter 5 we examine the basis of the PRC's claim to sovereign jurisdiction over Taiwan, which the PRC portrays as fixed and based on claims going back to antiquity. In much western coverage the provenance and development of China's claims are neglected entirely, taken for granted, treated as inexplicable, or merely as an example of authoritarian revisionism. In this chapter we show how Chinese claims are a relatively modern invention rooted in longer historical connections, how the PRC articulates its claim despite never having ruled Taiwan, and how Taiwanese sovereignty has become the intractable issue it is today. The goal of this chapter is to take the PRC's claims seriously in order to understand their goals and motivations. We explore how China uses Taiwan in various contexts to consolidate the PRC's claim and delegitimatize Taiwan's, including the framing of Taiwan to PRC publics, blocking Taiwan's participation in international organizations like the World Health Organization, and incentivizing governments and firms to adopt the Chinese government position. We also assess how the PRC has attempted to appeal to Taiwanese publics, through positive actions such as preferential visas and work opportunities, and "grey zone" activity such as media influence and propaganda.

US–Taiwan relations have significantly shaped the US–China relationship. How this geopolitical triangle evolved is of central relevance, and the fact that for several decades it produced a liveable equilibrium was no small feat. Chapter 6 explains how the US took on such a central role in the "Taiwan question", from supporting the ROC during the Cold War through the normalization of relations with the PRC in the 1970s and economic engagement with China in the 1990s to the current position as nominal guarantor of Taiwanese security. We show how the US position on Taiwan is a product of its own strategic interests in the region and the broader evolution of US–China relations. US policy toward Taiwan, encoded in the One-China policy, various communiques and the Taiwan Relations Act (TRA), has been remarkably stable over the past four decades. We show how the TRA framework came into effect and demystify what is meant by the US' "One-China policy", in contradistinction to the PRC's "One-China principle". US policy toward Taiwan is also the product of political preferences within the US, which we briefly survey, including a disambiguation of political party and institutional preferences. We briefly characterize policies enacted by different American presidents and examine how Taiwanese leaders have responded to US policy and appealed to the US. We cover how Taiwan became a bipartisan issue while also exploring some of the challenges faced to maintaining this status. Finally, we explain how American support for Taiwan has become embedded in the concept and praxis of a "free and open Indo-Pacific" and maintenance of the "international rules-based order".

In Chapter 7 we assess the security situation in the Taiwan Strait from multiple perspectives. We describe the PLA's modernization, the US security architecture and Taiwan's efforts to defend itself. We explain how different actors understand Taiwanese security and how they prepare their own defence posture accordingly. Beyond the principal actors, we shall show how Japan, Australia and other interested parties factor into questions of regional security. A pressing question in policy circles is what a conflict over Taiwan might entail. We thus survey various conflict scenarios and degrees of conflict (from cyberwarfare through blockade to full-scale invasion and occupation). We summarize the various issues associated with a hypothetical forced annexation and assess the options for different actor responses. Taiwan's own domestic military capabilities are a key issue here, hence we shall assess Taiwan's preparedness, defensive capacities and the domestic political competition and debates around the issue. The assumption underpinning this chapter is that "peaceful unification" under the auspices of "one country, two systems" has minimal political currency in Taiwan, yet that does not mean that conflict is inevitable. Militarized conflict in the Taiwan Strait would be devastating and destabilizing on a global scale, and thus there are strong incentives to avoid it through engagement and management of differences.

Chapter 8 on Taiwan's political economy briefly sets out how Taiwan became a global trading economy and tech powerhouse at the centre of global semiconductor supply chains. We briefly situate Taiwan's economic development in the broader developmental experience of East Asia and demonstrate how economic liberalization on both sides of the Taiwan Strait fostered intense economic interaction. These processes created economic interdependencies that continue despite political and diplomatic difficulties. However, economic interdependence is not without risk for Taiwan, which saw many industries relocate to the PRC with its cheaper costs and investment incentives. The PRC has also made an explicit connection between economics and politics, leading many Taiwanese to fear the PRC's use of economic leverage to force Taiwan to the negotiating table to talk about unification. We discuss how triangular interdependencies between the US, China and Taiwan have changed over time, and speculate on the sustainability of trade and investment relations under the threat of military conflict. After surveying the position of Taiwan's economy in global and cross-Strait terms, the chapter zeroes in on Taiwan's domestic situation and the effect economic issues have on Taiwanese politics and society. Beyond just cross-Strait economics, Taiwan faces many issues common to advanced economies, in terms of inequality, social mobility, and cost of living, which are manifest in political divisions, social movements and a generational divide.

In Chapter 9 we situate the "Taiwan question" in the broader context of international relations, the emergence of a bifurcation in foreign relations between authoritarian and democratic political systems, and explain why Taiwan is so central to peace and development in the Asia-Pacific region and the world. The chapter looks at the internationalization of the Taiwan question and Taiwan's efforts to consolidate "para-diplomatic" relations and economic diversification. Although Taiwan is excluded from participating in most international organizations and has formal diplomatic relations with a mere handful of small nations, it enjoys extensive global interactions as the possessor of great economic and soft power. It is actively pursuing international trade deals and has its own ambitious multinational economic engagement plan in the form of the New Southbound Policy. The chapter shows how Taiwan is highly active in public diplomacy and uses its soft power reserves to navigate the limits imposed on its participation in international society.

Chapter 10 provides some informed speculation about the future direction of cross-Strait relations, Taiwan's domestic politics, and US–Taiwan relations. The goal of this chapter is not to offer definitive predictions, but to encourage readers to consider what some key possibilities might be given the current state of Taiwanese domestic and international politics. In synthesizing what the book has covered, we summarize the tools and analytical lenses now available to readers to better understand Taiwan's domestic and international politics, and most importantly the complex trilateral relationship between Taiwan, China and the United States. Although we do not believe that military conflict is inevitable, it is necessary to consider the circumstances under which conflict might occur, which we discuss in this concluding chapter.

2

Taiwan's many histories

There is no single grand history of Taiwan. Instead, there are many histories involving multiple peoples, civilizations and empires that have all at different times lived, thrived, or struggled on the islands of Taiwan. These histories are imperative to understanding contemporary Taiwan, but even scholars often lament the difficulty of succinctly retelling them. Taiwan has been ruled by the Portuguese, Dutch, Ming dynasty, Qing dynasty and the Japanese. From 1945 to the present day, it has existed as the Republic of China (ROC), which was founded in China in 1912 and existed there until 1949. For thousands of years before that, Taiwan was home to Indigenous peoples of Austronesian heritage, who are culturally and linguistically related to other Pacific Island cultures. Traders and pirates once made Taiwan one of the most important and diverse centres of commerce, and in the last 400 years people from all over Southeast and Northeast Asia – and periodically, Europeans – have called Taiwan home. Today, Taiwan's population is predominantly Han Chinese (over 95 per cent). But to describe Taiwan as a Han Chinese society would be to erase the multicultural mélange that has defined so much of Taiwan's history. The goal of this chapter is to explore some of this historical diversity, showing how various settlers, colonizers, and empires have shaped Taiwan, and how these forces are manifest today.

PREMODERN TAIWAN

Any history of Taiwan must begin by recognizing that Indigenous peoples lived and thrived on these islands long before any Chinese or western powers brought Taiwan into the world of modern geopolitics. At the same time, perhaps no other group has suffered more throughout each era of Taiwanese history than Indigenous peoples. Today, Indigenous Taiwanese make up a small percentage of the total population (around 2.5 per cent) due to centuries of colonialism, imperialism, and systemic oppression. But they continue to survive as complex contemporary peoples, and their relevance to Taiwan's history and politics today should not be understated.

Indigenous Taiwanese likely arrived in Taiwan over 4,000 years ago. By contrast, Han Chinese only began living in Taiwan around 400 years ago. Indigenous languages are Austronesian, unlike Sinitic Chinese languages, and based on linguistic clues anthropologists suspect that from Taiwan Austronesian peoples migrated as far as Hawaii and Madagascar (Ko *et al.* 2014). The 16 officially recognized Indigenous peoples within Taiwan are themselves extremely diverse.[1] Like Taiwanese history, there is no singular Indigenous history. Instead, each people's history varies greatly depending on geography, settlement area, relationship to other peoples, and experience with the various outside forces that have controlled Taiwan. For example, foreign colonizers primarily arrived in Taiwan via its West coast. Subsequently, Indigenous peoples on the western coastal plain experienced colonialism differently than those on the East coast separated by impassable mountains. After Taiwan's "discovery" by outside forces, Indigenous peoples were subject to violence, displacement and discrimination. It is only since democratization that Taiwan has recognized the central place of Indigenous peoples in Taiwan's history and the contribution of Indigenous cultures to the unique hybrid that is Taiwanese culture. In 2016, on behalf of the Taiwanese government, President Tsai Ing-wen formally apologized to Taiwan's Indigenous peoples for harms suffered through historical mistreatment (Chu & Huang 2021).

---

1. The 16 peoples or nations are the Amis (Pangcah), Atayal, Paiwan, Bunun, Puyuma, Rukai, Tsou, Saisiyat, Yami (Tao), Thao, Kavalan, Truku, Sakizaya, Seediq, Kla'alua and Kanakanavu.

TAIWAN BECOMES PART OF THE CHINESE EMPIRE

The story of how Taiwan was integrated into dynastic China paradoxically begins with the Dutch. When the Dutch began to arrive in Taiwan in 1624, Taiwan had not yet been incorporated into imperial China, or any other empire. Although the Portuguese began using the name *Ihla Formosa* ("the beautiful island") to describe Taiwan, among European powers it was the Dutch that established the most solid presence in Taiwan. Primarily based in southern Taiwan close to modern day Tainan, seventeenth-century Dutch colonial forts remain major tourist attractions. The Dutch East India Company invested heavily in Taiwan in order to compete with other European powers active in East Asia. The Portuguese had Macao, the Spanish had the Philippines, and the Dutch chose Taiwan. The Dutch were the first outside power to attempt to control the whole of Taiwan. However, while they did exert control over the most populated parts of the island at the time, they never established authority over the entire island. The Dutch approach was not settler colonialism, and thus Dutch citizens were not brought in large numbers to populate Taiwan. Instead, small numbers of Dutch soldiers, administrators and traders formed a privileged elite who ruled over the local population through the Dutch East India Company.

Who were the local populations at this time? Indigenous Taiwanese were certainly present, but so were an increasing number of Han Chinese who were moving to Taiwan from southern China. Japanese and Southeast Asian fisherman and agricultural workers also found their way to Taiwan. Along with its Dutch and Portuguese merchants, seventeenth-century Taiwan was already a diverse and multicultural island. West coast Indigenous peoples had a contentious but steady trade partnership with early Dutch settlers and colonists. The Dutch attempted to recruit Indigenous Taiwanese as labourers, but were largely unsuccessful in convincing them to abandon their existing ways of life. It was the Dutch colonizers' need for labour, and the refusal of Indigenous Taiwanese to provide it, that precipitated Han Chinese migration to Taiwan from Ming dynasty China.

Pirates were also frequent visitors to Taiwan. Piracy had long been present in East Asia before the 1600s, and Taiwan's convenient geographic location made it a frequent port of call and base for pirates from all over the world. One such pirate, Zheng Zhi-long, was a frequent trader with the Dutch. His relationship with the Europeans was so good that he eventually converted to Christianity and took the name Nicholas Gaspard. In 1624, Zheng Zhilong and his Japanese wife Tagawa Matsu had a son named Zheng Chenggong, better known today as Koxinga. Raised around piracy and the Dutch, Koxinga nonetheless became a scholar and member of the Ming dynasty court. However, the Ming dynasty was in decline and the Ming court's Han-run government was losing authority over China. A challenger, in the form of a Manchu government from Northeast China, was rapidly expanding its own rule under the auspices of the Qing dynasty. As a Ming loyalist, Koxinga recruited his father to use his pirate fleet to help fight on behalf of the Ming. When the balance of power shifted in favour of the insurgent Qing, Zheng Zhilong switched sides to the Qing, but his son Koxinga remained a Ming loyalist. After his father's death, Koxinga inherited his family's wealth and power and used it to fight one last battle against the Qing – which he lost.

Koxinga and his personal navy fleet fled to Taiwan. Despite his family's long-time ties with the Dutch, he attacked the European colonialists and eventually defeated them, ending their time in Taiwan. When Koxinga arrived, he officially intertwined Taiwan and its future into the politics of the Chinese empire. Although some narratives point to this moment as representing the absorption of Taiwan by the Ming dynasty, the Ming at this juncture was in the terminal stage of decline and barely functional. Foreshadowing Chiang Kai-shek's Nationalists in the twentieth century, Koxinga envisaged Taiwan as a base for recouping his forces and launching a bid to retake China and restore the Ming. Unfortunately for Koxinga, the majority of his officers and soldiers defected to the Qing, which offered amnesty if they surrendered. After a couple decades, the Qing defeated Koxinga and officially took control of Taiwan. It is from the time of the Manchu Qing dynasty – the final dynasty of imperial China – that Taiwan was considered to be part of China's territory.

When Koxinga initially arrived in Taiwan he had brought with him tens of thousands of Han Chinese, many of whom settled in Taiwan. This migration dramatically altered the composition of Taiwan's population and the power dynamics of the various ethnic groups that lived on the island. Under Koxinga, Han Chinese became the new privileged class and began to further Sinicize Indigenous Taiwanese. Many scholars conceptualize Koxinga's regime as a form of Chinese settler colonialism that was subsequently continued for centuries by the Qing.

TAIWAN AND THE QING DYNASTY

Although Taiwan was incorporated into the Qing dynasty in 1684 as a three-county prefecture administered by Fujian province, it was not formally designated a province of China until some 200 years later in 1887. After defeating Koxinga, the Qing court remained sceptical about the utility of keeping Taiwan. As the Veritable Records of the Kangxi Emperor of the Qing in 1683 put it: "Taiwan is no bigger than a ball of mud. We gain nothing by possessing it, and it would be no loss if we did not acquire it" (Teng 2004: 34). Shi Lang, a naval commander who helped lead the efforts against Koxinga, eventually persuaded the emperor that controlling Taiwan suited the Qing's interests. Indeed, the Qing was an expansionary dynasty that would eventually expand China's borders to incorporate territories never before considered part of China, including Taiwan.

Like the Dutch, the Qing also never had full control over both West and East coasts of the island. Qing rule was restricted to the West, and the East was such an afterthought that many early Qing maps do not bother depicting that part of the island. Eastern Taiwan was not even considered part of Qing territory. Infamously, when the USS Rover crashed on the eastern coast of Taiwan in 1867, and the crew was killed by Indigenous Taiwanese, the Qing denied responsibility since "the Americans were not killed on Chinese territory" (Teng 2004: 210).

By the late 1700s, Taiwan's Han population already significantly exceeded the Indigenous population, with some estimates citing around 800,000 Han to 40,000 Indigenous people (Brown 2004: 40). The Qing's colonial expansion into Taiwan made it an agricultural trade hub. Taiwan became a major source of rice and sugarcane for China and was often referred to by Qing elites as the "Granary of China". But global forces also had their eye on Taiwan. Imperial European, Japanese and American powers were increasingly interested in expanding trade access in East Asia, and all eyed Taiwan as a pivotal port island.

Han Chinese men, rather than women, were more likely to migrate to Taiwan and once there the level of intermarriage with Indigenous Taiwanese was high. With direct and often forced integration into Qing settlements, Indigenous peoples in the West of the island gradually became Sinicized and assimilated into Qing cultural practices. More isolated peoples on the East coast were better able to resist assimilation. From a geographical perspective, gaining entry to Taiwan's East coast was challenging. A high mountain range divides the island down the middle and the eastern seaboard is less conducive to the construction of ports or agricultural settlements. As a result, neither the Dutch nor the Qing colonists were able to settle the East coast of Taiwan.

With no foreign entity trying to control the East coast, Indigenous peoples there were able to maintain their traditional practices longer than their counterparts on the rest of the island. Qing settlers used racially pejorative terms to describe this difference, referring to Indigenous peoples on the West coast as "cooked" and those on the East as "raw" because of their different levels of cultural assimilation (Hsieh 2017). Not all Indigenous people on the West coast were assimilated. Many Indigenous peoples were pushed out of their homes on the West coast and forced inland across the mountains and eventually to the East coast. A demographic map of contemporary Taiwan shows most Indigenous Taiwanese living on the East coast, but this is not by choice. Rather, it represents a forced relocation unfolding over several centuries.

It was a combination of lack of authority over the East coast and the fear of other imperial powers coveting Taiwan that ultimately pushed the Qing into designating Taiwan a province of China. Japanese explorers had begun to explore and map the Eastern Coast, hinting at ambitions to take control of East Taiwan. The Qing worried that if they did not claim Eastern Taiwan as their territory other powers, especially Japan, would attempt to claim it, potentially destabilizing Qing control over the rest of Taiwan. The Qing enacted a new colonial policy called "Opening the Mountains and Pacifying the Savages" (Teng 2004). This policy would facilitate unification of the island under Qing control, albeit with incomplete control of the East Coast, through the forced Sinicization of Indigenous Taiwanese.

Aside from the actions of the Japanese, French forces unsuccessfully attempted to seize Taiwan from the Qing during the Sino-French War of

1884. It became clear to the Qing that designating Taiwan as more than just a border territory was necessary to forestall further such efforts. Thus in 1887, the Qing officially declared Taiwan a province under their jurisdiction.

THE JAPANESE COLONIAL ERA

Taiwan's formal status as a Chinese province under the Qing lasted a mere eight years. In 1895, when the defeated Qing signed the Treaty of Shimonoseki to end the first Sino-Japanese War, Taiwan was ceded in perpetuity to Japan, becoming a colony of the growing Japanese imperial empire. A small number of provincial officials loyal to the Qing resisted the new colonial arrangements, uniting in 1895 to declare a short-lived independent Republic of Formosa (Lamley 1968). They fled from Taipei to Tainan as soon as the Japanese army arrived, and their independent republic lasted a mere five months before dissolving. A strange and largely inconsequential historical footnote to most, it is nevertheless celebrated by some as the first attempt to establish an independent republic on Taiwan.

For the first three years of Japanese rule the military police strictly governed the island, quashing sporadic acts of resistance. After these transitional years, a formal Japanese colonial government was installed and took full control of the entire island for the first time. Compared with the brutal colonization of Northeastern China and Korea, Taiwan's experience as a Japanese colony was less bloody and repressive. Taiwanese were required to learn Japanese, adapt to Japan's education system, and adopt many Japanese cultural practices. The legacies of these experiences are still in evidence today. For example, many words in Taiwanese Hokkien are loan words taken from the Japanese colonial era. While most Taiwanese subjects of Japanese colonialism did not suffer as badly as people in other areas, the same cannot be said for Taiwan's Indigenous peoples. Although some Indigenous peoples cooperated with the Japanese colonial administration, others resisted, often leading to brutal massacres.

Japan's ambition for Taiwan was to establish it as a "model colony", an example to show off to the rest of the world that it too could succeed as

Taiwan

an imperial power (Heé 2014). The incentive was to demonstrate to the western imperial powers that Japan was equally capable of creating and maintaining a colonial state. Taiwan became a point of pride for Japan because of its success as a colony. Under Japanese rule, Taiwan was also integrated into the global economy of the time. Taiwan's modernization, including land and education reform, and other key parts of state development began during the Japanese colonial era and their legacies can still be felt in Taiwan today. Even though Taiwanese were treated as an inferior class to the Japanese colonizers, civil society also had its antecedents under Japanese rule. Taiwanese citizens were allowed very limited political participation and no meaningful power or influence, but the shoots of a Taiwanese political identity can be traced to the period (Lin 2022).

The formation of a unique Taiwanese identity connected with a push for Taiwanese self-determination is highly salient in contemporary democratic Taiwan. But the first manifestation of this phenomenon can be traced to the Japanese colonial era. When some well-off and well-connected Taiwanese families were able to send their children to school in Japan, some of them were exposed to anti-imperialist literature and texts on self-determination. Embryonic student movements began to form in both Japan and Taiwan that were rooted in resistance to Japanese colonialism and the notion of "Taiwan for Taiwanese" (Hsiao 2003). The fact that these earliest student movements involved "privileged" young Taiwanese is a reminder that all Taiwanese, relatively well-off or not, were second-class citizens under Japanese colonial rule. These student movements were limited in their ability to bring about meaningful political or social change, but their legacy and writings would become a source of motivation and inspiration for later Taiwanese independence activists and social movements.

Like the western imperial powers it sought to emulate, Japanese colonial regimes utilized discriminatory logics to govern racial diversity among subject peoples. Despite its status as a "model colony", Taiwan did not escape this fate. Japanese considered themselves a superior race, with inferior Han Chinese a class below. A further level below that, Taiwan's Indigenous peoples were objectified as "backwards" and "savage", the opposite of "civilized" Japanese people. The forced relocation of Indigenous peoples that had begun during the Qing dynasty continued under Japanese rule. Indigenous peoples that resisted faced violent repression. During one episode described as the Musha Incident, the Seediq Indigenous people rebelled against the Japanese, killing over 100 soldiers. Japanese reprisals led to the murder of 600 Seediq people. Eventually the rebellion was quelled, and Seediq lands were distributed to Indigenous peoples that did not rebel against the Japanese. Pitting Indigenous groups against each other was another characteristic of Japanese rule.

Once Japan gained full authority over the entire island, Han and Indigenous Taiwanese alike became colonial subjects of Japan's empire and were educated as such (Tsurumi 1977). Such was the spread of Japanese culture and language in an attempt to nurture a sense of "Japaneseness", that during the Second World War Han and Indigenous Taiwanese volunteered in large numbers to join their conscripted counterparts in fighting for Japan. It is hard to parse loyalty to Japan from other possible motivations, but contemporaneous accounts do suggest widespread acceptance of Japanese colonial rule after some time (Ching 2001).

TRANSITION TO ROC RULE

While Taiwan was growing socially and economically under Japanese colonial rule, China under the Qing was going through a period of intense political volatility. As the decline of the Qing dynasty accelerated, warlords and other political factions attempted to establish and consolidate their claim to represent a new legitimate ruling body for China. In 1911, disillusioned with the failing Qing dynasty, Sun Yat-sen founded the Republic of China (Schiffrin 1970). The ROC to Sun was a Han-centric government embodying what he saw as fundamental Chinese values. The story of the ROC and its relationship to Taiwan is covered in more depth in Chapter 4. Here, the point that matters is that the ROC was recognized as the legitimate governing body of China. Between 1912 and 1949, the ROC, despite various periods of weakened authority, legitimacy and capacity, was the official government of China.

At the Cairo Conference in 1943 near the end of the Second World War, the US and UK told the leader of the ROC, Chiang Kai-shek, that

Taiwan had been taken from China by Japan and it would be restored to the ROC. Following Japan's surrender, Taiwan was formally incorporated into the ROC in 1945. Many Taiwanese were optimistic and even hopeful about the ROC and the Nationalist KMT government that would replace the Japanese colonial rulers. The transition, however, was chaotic and violent. The Nationalists, by now busy fighting the rump of the Japanese occupying forces and Mao's Red Army, expected an easy transition to governing Taiwan. What they found was a society that had spent the last 50 years assimilating to Japanese rule, not a population of Chinese citizens familiar with life in Republican China. Hardly anyone in Taiwan spoke Mandarin, a language from northern China, at least as a first language. Taiwanese people spoke Taiwanese Hokkien, Hakka, Indigenous languages or Japanese. Taiwanese elites in Taipei, who spoke mostly Japanese and had managed to secure a small degree of power under the colonial regime, expected that the KMT would welcome their help with the governing transition. But Taiwanese elites were not seen as "Chinese" by KMT/ROC standards, one characteristic of which was enmity toward the Japanese. The new KMT/ROC regime thus set itself the task of ridding Taiwanese of their sense of "Japaneseness" and instilling a sense of "Chineseness" in its place.

Taiwanese citizens quickly realized their optimism for the ROC was misplaced. In 1946, Japanese and Taiwanese Hokkien were made illegal, and Mandarin was mandated the new national language, despite most people in Taiwan still being unable to speak it fluently. A clear social hierarchy formed between the two million or so largely Han Chinese who evacuated to Taiwan with the KMT from 1945 until 1949 and the Han Chinese population whose settlement on Taiwan pre-dated the Japanese colonial period. The divide between the newcomers (*waishengren*, literally "people from outside the province") and those who already lived in Taiwan (*benshengren*, literally "people from this province") became a salient political and social cleavage. During the early decades of the ROC regime in Taiwan, *waishengren* constituted an elite class enjoying privileges above *benshengren* and Indigenous peoples. Within a year of the ROC taking control of Taiwan, discontent and anger towards the KMT government had grown among Taiwanese people.

THE 228 INCIDENT AND WHITE TERROR

The most consequential event in modern Taiwanese history is known as the 228 incident (read *two-two-eight* reflecting the date "February 28"). This critical juncture led indirectly to 38 years of martial law and became a catalyst for Taiwanese subjectivity and identity (Edmondson 2002). The proximate cause of the 228 incident was relatively innocuous. On 27 February 1947, an elderly woman was selling illegal cigarettes next to the Tobacco and Liquor Monopoly Bureau in Taipei. When police officers employed by the ROC state went to arrest her, a crowd of ordinary Taiwanese formed in her defence. An officer hit the woman when she resisted arrest and a scuffle ensued. In the confusion, a bystander was shot by police. Word of the incident spread quickly across the island. Although the propaganda commissioner ordered the media not to report on what occurred, the next day, 28 February, hundreds of protesters gathered at the Provincial Administration Executive Office. Intimidated by the protesters, members of the ragtag police force opened fire randomly, killing two and wounding many more bystanders.

Throughout the next week anti-government protests erupted around the island. Because the majority of the KMT's fighting forces were still in China fighting the civil war, local Taiwanese were briefly able to assert nominal control of Taiwan. A Taiwan Resolution Committee was established in Taipei with the ambition of negotiating for better treatment of Taiwanese citizens with the KMT. Once KMT reinforcements arrived, however, any possibility of reconciliation evaporated.

Beginning on 7 March, KMT-directed Nationalist army troops arrived on the island and a crackdown immediately ensued. In the cities, soldiers fired indiscriminately at civilians (Smith 2008 148). Members of the Resolution Committee, protest leaders and organizers and other Taiwanese elites were targeted. The violence lasted until 15 March. Estimates of the total number of Taiwanese killed falls between 20,000 and 30,000 people (Smith 2008: 150). Having re-established control through a week of physical violence, the KMT would then unleash a decades-long period of systematic political repression known as the "White Terror". The era of White Terror in Taiwan largely overlaps with the period of martial law. Although a strict government crackdown started immediately after the 228 incident, martial law was not enforced

23

formally until 19 May 1949 when Chiang Kai-shek arrived in Taiwan. It lasted until 15 July 1987, constituting one of the longest periods of martial law anywhere in the world.

Under martial law the KMT governed Taiwan as an authoritarian single-party government. Personal and social freedoms were limited. Still effectively on a war-footing and paranoid of communist infiltration, the KMT created a highly effective police state. *Waishengren* were not excluded from being closely monitored and targeted by the KMT government, despite their status as a privileged class. Any suspicion of anti-KMT sentiment could place an individual and their family at risk of arrest or worse. It is estimated that over 140,000 people were imprisoned, and 3,000–4,000 executed for alleged anti-KMT crimes.

The centrality of the 228 incident and White Terror for contemporary Taiwanese identity cannot be overstated (Shih & Chen 2010). The White Terror era and the 228 incident can still be a source of division. Pan-green perspectives (i.e. on the Democratic Progressive Party (DPP) side of the political spectrum) emphasize an act of ethnic violence against *benshengren* and decades of martial law that structurally and violently oppressed those who opposed KMT rule. Pan-blue (i.e. the KMT side of the spectrum) perspectives contend that the crackdown was justified by mass civil unrest, note that *waishengren* were also victims of the White Terror, or even suggest that the whole affair was purposely started by communist agents provocateurs.

Under martial law the 228 incident was taboo and could not be discussed in public. It is only since democratization and protections of free speech that Taiwanese people have been able to discuss the violence experienced across generations during martial law. Contemporary transitional justice efforts have largely focused on truth and reconciliation from the White Terror era and is a fertile topic of research in Taiwan Studies.

During the martial law era, Taiwanese culture and society underwent extensive transformation. Taiwanese identity became heavily Chinese-centric thanks to KMT reforms to the education system. By making Mandarin language and Chinese history core components of the national school curriculum, and enforcing compliance through direct and indirect coercion, the KMT instilled a sense of ROC Chineseness in generations of Taiwanese people (Chun 1994). Land reforms, state-led industrialization, and an export-oriented economic model facilitated rapid and equitable economic growth in Taiwan. By the late 1970s, led by the KMT's authoritarian developmental state model, Taiwan had become a player in the global economy.

Despite systematically repressive and periodically brutal authoritarian rule, the KMT oversaw economic reform, education reform, and the growth of civil society similar to that of the Japanese colonial era. A number of KMT policy programmes such as land reform built on the Japanese colonial era policies (Ho 1987). These government-driven growth and reform policies coupled with slowly allowing civil society to grow were all precursors to Taiwan's eventual democratization.

Contemporary Taiwanese civil society often compares and contrasts the Japanese colonial era and the KMT authoritarian era, often along partisan lines. For some, the Japanese colonial era is remembered fondly because of the perception that the Japanese treated Taiwanese less cruelly than the KMT. For others, the KMT authoritarian era is seen as a necessary step in Taiwan's political development, and that nostalgia for Japanese colonialism risks romanticizing or revising a cruel part of Taiwanese history. The complexities and passions evoked by these debates reflect how experiences in Taiwanese history are contested and remain unavoidable influences on contemporary political and national identity (Lin 2022).

During the martial law era, the KMT began to develop Indigenous communities on Taiwan's East Coast. Even though Indigenous Taiwanese peoples were discriminated against by the KMT, this marked the beginning of the Taiwanese government investing in their communities. Subject to Sinicization like the rest of Taiwan, many Indigenous communities felt that at least the KMT was providing services to them in a way that gained their political trust. As a result, the KMT cultivated political trust and support, and for many years Indigenous Taiwanese voted predominantly for the KMT (Simon 2010).

DEMOCRATIZATION

In 1975, Chiang Kai-shek, the long-time authoritarian leader of the KMT died. His son, Chiang Ching-kuo eventually succeeded him in becoming ROC president in 1978. Taiwan remained a single-party system under martial law. The state's mass surveillance system continued to operate, individual rights were still limited and contingent, and the political status of the numerical minority *waishengren* was still superior to the majority *benshengren*. Yet, civil society in Taiwan was growing and changing, and would soon represent a challenge to the new Chiang regime.

Taiwan's equitable economic growth (discussed in Chapter 8) had produced a large and well-educated middle class, which cut across ethnic lines. People were increasingly invested in "political questions" and starting to become more outspoken in their feelings about Taiwan's future. Without understating the stubbornly authoritarian nature of the KMT state, Taiwan was slowly becoming more liberalized, and these societal changes were reflected under Chiang Ching-kuo's rule. Society was more open than under Chiang Kai-shek, and a limited amount of public dissent against the KMT was tolerated. The party itself had "indigenized", welcoming wealthy or influential *benshengren* into its ranks. Some even become high-ranking members of the KMT. The extent to which Chiang Ching-kuo should be credited for liberalizing Taiwan, and how much was due to bottom-up actions in civil society and other factors, has long been debated by scholars.

Dissent against the KMT began with a movement called the *tangwai* (also spelled *dangwai*), which literally means "outside the party". Since organized political opposition was illegal under martial law, *tangwai* described an identity and a loose affiliation. *Tangwai* figures held diverse political views, the only consistent stance being opposition to the KMT's authoritarianism (Chiou 1986). It is wrong to describe the *tangwai* as a solely pro-Taiwan independence movement, although numerous *tangwai* figures were pro-independence. Most activists within the *tangwai* were pro-democracy and wanted to see the ROC transition from an authoritarian polity to a democratic one. Other *tangwai* factions advocated for self-determination, meaning they wanted Taiwanese citizens to have the right to decide Taiwan's future. And some *tangwai* sought Taiwan's independence from the ROC by replacing it with a hypothetical Republic of Taiwan.

Tangwai were divided over the choice of pushing for change from within the system or employing more confrontational methods. Limited space and tools were available under authoritarian rule. Non-KMT members were permitted to stand for city-council and other low-level electoral offices as independent candidates, and early *tangwai* members competed for and sometimes won such seats. Other *tangwai* felt that the best way to exert pressure on the KMT was through grassroots organizing and street protests against the authoritarian state. These fundamental divides in political goals, tactics, and relations to each other made the *tangwai* a loose and fractious entity. Although they shared the goal of political reform, factions disagreed and fought with each other over how to achieve change (Chou & Nathan 1987).

One of the most consequential events of Taiwan's early democratization period, and a key source of *tangwai* coherence and momentum, was the Meilidao or Kaohsiung Incident in December 1979. Two *tangwai* leaders, Shih Ming-teh and Huang Hsin-chieh, had founded a pro-democracy magazine called *Formosa* (*Meilidao* in Chinese), which served as a popular vehicle for activists and advocates. The KMT had allowed some small-scale opposition events to take place, but *Formosa's* proposal for a march to celebrate Human Rights Day was too much for the KMT authorities. Denied a permit for the protest, *Formosa's* editors decided to hold the event in their offices in Taiwan's second biggest city, the southern port of Kaohsiung. The police closed the event down, clashing with participants and arresting *tangwai* leaders. The KMT seized on the incident to launch a wider crackdown on the *tangwai*.

The Kaohsiung Incident became an important catalyst for the democracy movement in Taiwan, mobilizing activists and inspiring action. *Tangwai* activism grew quickly and spread widely in the early 1980s in response to the KMT's repression. The KMT itself, by then a party with many *benshengren* officials and members, saw signs of liberalization and permitted further loosening of Taiwan's stringent laws. One of the key KMT leaders, Lee Teng-hui, who would serve as ROC president from 1988 to 2000, was among the KMT elites who favoured liberalization.

In September 1986, *tangwai* activists gathered at an unlikely venue. The Grand Hotel in Taipei is a neoclassical Chinese architectural extravagance built for Chiang Kai-shek to entertain foreign leaders as ROC president. The *tangwai* leaders were there to formally establish an opposition political party: the Democratic Progressive Party (DPP). Despite opposition parties being illegal under martial law, the KMT tacitly accepted the DPP's existence and allowed its members to compete in supplementary elections for the legislature later that year. A year later, martial law was officially rescinded and the momentum towards democratization was becoming inexorable. By 1991, Taiwan held its first semi-democratic election for the National Assembly, and five years later Taiwanese citizens participated in Taiwan's first free and fair election of the ROC president. Thus began the period of democratic Taiwan (Wachman 1994).

Democratization processes created the political landscape that characterizes Taiwan today, with the big-tent DPP and KMT parties competing alongside smaller niche parties. In the next chapter we discuss how Taiwan became a democracy, how Taiwanese people vote and why they support certain parties.

3

Decided by the Taiwanese people

Contemporary Taiwan is a democracy with strong institutions, an independent judiciary, free media, and routine free and fair elections. Political participation is high, with keenly fought campaigns and intense political debates. There are features in the operation and practice of democracy in Taiwan that older democracies could learn from. Every citizen has the right to vote, ballots are counted efficiently and publicly to ensure accountability, and civil society is bustling with watchdog organizations to track parties and politicians during elections. The institutions that make up Taiwan's democracy were forged through decades of authoritarian rule and subsequent democratization processes (Rigger 2002), and in some respects democratic reforms are still incomplete and ongoing (Mattlin 2011). In this chapter, we will summarize the main features of Taiwan's democratic transition, discuss how Taiwan's democracy works today, and explore the unique political spectrum that defines everyday politics.

THE CAUSES OF TAIWAN'S DEMOCRATIZATION

Democratization in Taiwan was a gradual, generally peaceful and multi-faceted process extending over a prolonged period and marked by electoral milestones (Tien & Chu 1996). It generally followed a cycle of opposition demands for reform, concessions by the KMT, followed by further demands from civil society. Democratization is not simple anywhere and Taiwan was no exception. The extent of the KMT's authoritarian rule under martial law was so ubiquitous that every sector, every institution and the entire bureaucracy required liberalizing reforms.

What led to Taiwan's democratization? What were the necessary conditions that allowed for Taiwan to democratize after decades of authoritarian rule? There is no singular cause or single answer. Instead, there are a host of important factors that together led to Taiwan's democratic transition. While many different theories of democratization may emphasize the role of the KMT or the role of grassroots activists, it was a combination of these different variables that pushed Taiwan to democratize. We summarize these conditions here.

First, physical infrastructure established during the Japanese colonial era and KMT authoritarian era. Despite relegating Taiwanese people to second-class citizens, Japanese colonial rule was responsible for beginning Taiwan's industrialization process. Physical infrastructure like railroads, wells and irrigation for agriculture were constructed across Taiwan. During the KMT authoritarian era, the government benefited from these foundations, expanding and modernizing infrastructure for industry, agriculture and transport. It was these institutional developments and reforms on which all other subsequent civil society and government advancement were built on.

Second, education standardization and reform under Japanese and KMT control. Education under Japanese rule was standardized and established for all Taiwanese, including Indigenous peoples. During KMT control, despite the Chinese nationalistic bias to the curriculum, literacy rates increased dramatically. The KMT's reverence for traditional Chinese cultural traits, the need to educate Taiwanese in the ways of the ROC and the government's pursuit of rapid industrialization (which required workers with a good general education) all contributed to a concentration on education. Expansion of compulsory education and a coherent national education system increased levels of education in Taiwan to an internationally high level.

Third, election experience during the Japanese and KMT eras. Taiwanese did not enjoy any sort of meaningful political representation or power during Japanese colonial rule. And under KMT authoritarian rule opportunities for political participation were limited and contingent. However, non-KMT members were eventually permitted to run for low-level positions like city councillors. Yet, despite their explicitly non-democratic political systems, both the Japanese and KMT regimes convened regular limited but meaningful elections. This experience established the practice and memory of voting for Taiwanese people even when living under a non-democratic government.

Fourth, increasing economic prosperity and equality. Taiwan's industrialization and modernization is a more complicated story than the "economic miracle" of the 1960s and 1970s. Taiwan enjoyed periods of significant growth under the Japanese and early KMT, but due to the nature of those regimes the benefits of economic development were not equally distributed. However, by the 1970s the KMT allowed upward mobility for non-KMT and non-*waishengren* Taiwanese and growth was more equally distributed. One of the major results was the growth of a large Taiwanese middle class, which was also highly educated, as noted above, and increasingly engaged in civil society. People could participate in clubs, travel and learn about the world beyond Taiwan. The ability for people to associate with different organizations, even those that were not political, helped build experience, norms and demands for political participation.

Fifth, some liberal reformers within the KMT. Democratization in Taiwan involved top-down and bottom-up pressures. Within the KMT regime there were reformers, including Chiang Ching-kuo, who perceived the limited lifespan of the authoritarian regime and the necessity to liberalize. Recent scholarship argues that it was because Chiang Ching-kuo saw the KMT in a position of strength that he was open to the idea of liberalizing, since he anticipated that KMT would still be able to maintain its power after democratization (Slater & Wong 2022). President Lee Teng-hui was another key KMT reformer who pushed for democratization, and there were numerous KMT elites who saw the importance of liberalizing Taiwanese civil society. Among them were some of the *benshengren* who had managed to climb the ranks of the KMT and push for reform from within. But there was also a current within the KMT that was confident the party could control the way democratization proceeded and ensure that the KMT would continue to prosper post-democratization.

Sixth, a non-violent opposition movement. The *tangwai* were the main channel through which civil society was able to advocate for democratization. Although a loose organization with different political goals and ideologies, *tangwai* involvement in protest against the KMT's authoritarianism and participation in low-level elections were fundamental to generating momentum towards democratization. An important aspect contributing to the *tangwai*'s effectiveness was the willingness to work within the system. Moderates within the *tangwai*, who saw the value of using formal institutions to push for reform, were able to cultivate relations with some members of the KMT, despite the party's initial strong opposition to democratization.

Finally, American political pressure. One issue that does not feature centrally in contemporary debates about US–Taiwan relations is American complicity in the KMT authoritarian government's oppressive regime. The KMT's staunch anti-communism made it a Cold War ally, and the US tolerated KMT repression while employing defence and trade policies that would help the regime entrench its power. The US largely turned a blind eye to the KMT's treatment of Taiwanese citizens during the martial law era. However, by the 1980s, amid the "Third Wave" of democratization, the US government began to change its tone. Rather than endorse the KMT's authoritarian regime, it began to communicate the desirability of liberalization and eventual democratization in Taiwan. The US was unable to unilaterally demand the KMT embrace democracy, but it did possess the policy levers and influence to encourage the party to move in that direction.

Taiwan's democratization was a combination of these different variables (Cheng 1989) and statements implying monocausality or suggesting a determinative role for Chiang Ching-kuo, Lee Teng-hui or the *tangwai* fail to capture complex antecedent conditions and contingent processes. Even the list above is not exhaustive, and Taiwan historians and political scientists continue to debate what other factors were part of the necessary conditions that allowed for Taiwan's democratic transition.

INDEPENDENCE AND UNIFICATION IN TAIWANESE POLITICS

Unlike many societies in Europe and North America, where political attitudes are typically defined by a left–right spectrum reflecting attitudes towards the role of governments and markets, the fundamental political question in Taiwan revolves around its relationship with China (Chu 2000). This question defines how people perceive and participate in politics, including how they vote. Instead of a left–right political spectrum defined by words like "liberal" or "conservative", Taiwan's dominant political span has "independence" at one end and "unification" at the other. In the terrain between these two poles is some version of the "status quo". This broad characterization masks many gradations and nuances, and connections to national identity, which we examine later in this chapter.

Before dissecting these preferences in a more granular way, here is a stylized version of the independence–unification preference structure. Independence broadly means support for Taiwan's formal statehood, namely a preference for Taiwan to be formally recognized as a *de jure* state under the name Taiwan. Those who support unification embrace the concept of "One China" and see Taiwan as inevitably tied to China. Among unification supporters, the major debate is which government would rule One China and what political system a unified single China would employ. Those who support the "status quo" – the majority of opinion poll respondents – are harder to pin down. Little data exists on how survey respondents understand what the "status quo" represents. However, we can say that it indicates that they do not want a formal change in Taiwan's current status, at least for now. They might support a *de facto* independence that is not formally recognized by most countries in the world. Or they might tolerate the status quo, because to change it would either lead to war (the independence option) or being subsumed by the PRC (the unification option). Perhaps they prefer to "wait and see", keeping their options open and observing what happens.

Contrary to portrayals of Taiwanese politics that present a simple "unification versus independence" binary, the preference structure is actually quite complex and contains many nuanced positions. "Independence" itself contains different variations. For some, independence equals a hypothetical Republic of Taiwan. Commonly called *Taidu*, the goal of this type of independence is to remove all remnants of the ROC from Taiwan. Constructing a hypothetical Republic of Taiwan would require writing a new constitution and establishing new political institutions, actions that the PRC credibly says would trigger war. For others, independence is formal recognition of the Republic of China as a state. Rather than eliminating the ROC and building a new state, supporters of what is referred to as the *Huadu* variation on independence want the ROC as it exists to become a formal member of the global order.

Unification also contains gradations. Those who support the idea of "blue unification" agree that unification is desirable, but only after the democratization of China, or when the KMT is able to regain control of China. As long as China exists as an authoritarian country, they do not support the idea of unification and prefer living in a democratic Republic of China, albeit restricted to Taiwan. Proponents of "red unification" advocate immediate unification with the PRC. They would be happy for Taiwan to be ruled by the PRC government and see unification as the only peaceful way for Taiwan to continue to exist.

To support the status quo also involves diverse preferences. Some people who support the status quo want some form of independence (either *Taidu* independence or *Huadu* independence) at a future juncture. Supporters of this position may want independence in principle, but due to Taiwan's contested position recognize that pursuing independence is too dangerous. Others support the status quo for now and want the freedom to decide on Taiwan's status at a later time. Supporters of this position have not decided if independence or unification is ultimately better for Taiwan (or more desirable for themselves as individuals), but feel the need to see what the future holds. Until then, the status quo of functional autonomy is the more flexible option.

How do Taiwanese people feel about these various positions? The Election Study Center at National Chengchi University in Taiwan has been polling Taiwanese public opinion on this question for nearly three decades.[1] Figure 3.1 shows the distribution of preferences over time.

In the survey, Taiwanese citizens can select among seven choices. These options do not encompass all possible positions and permutations, but the data can still tell us a number of important features about Taiwanese people's preferences over time.

First, the majority of Taiwanese people support some version of the status quo. Whether or not the status quo should stay as it is "indefinitely" or move toward unification or independence in the future does vary across time. How they understand the "status quo" is unfortunately not measured by this survey question, but the numbers tell us

---

1. See, https://esc.nccu.edu.tw/PageDoc/Detail?fid=7801&id=6963.

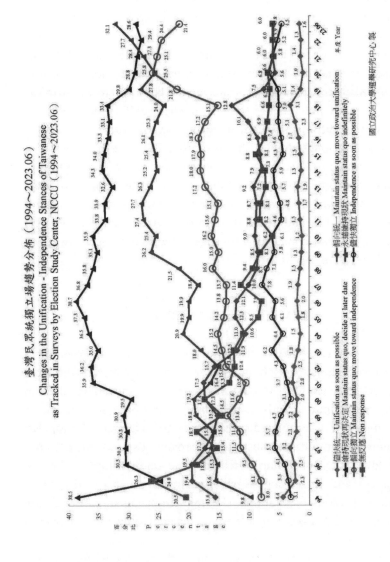

Figure 3.1 National status preferences over time

Source: Election Study Center, National Chengchi University

that Taiwanese people continue to be pragmatic about Taiwan's future national status. Rather than seeking immediate changes in Taiwan's position through independence or unification, they prefer to maintain Taiwan's contested status. This choice allows Taiwanese to maintain their de facto sovereignty and autonomy while avoiding risks to their democratic way of life.

Second, support for immediate and irremediable changes to the status quo, whether in the form of independence or unification, is low. That "immediate independence", which would likely lead to war with the PRC, consistently polls higher than "immediate unification" says a lot about Taiwanese attitudes toward accepting PRC overtures or bowing to PRC threats. Although the PRC has promised Taiwan a "high degree of autonomy" under "one country, two systems", very few Taiwanese support Taiwan becoming part of the PRC, at least in the immediate term. Polling even shows that Taiwan sees the PRC government as undesirable, even if some Taiwanese identify culturally with China. As a political system, the PRC as a choice for Taiwanese citizens is an option without appeal (Rigger *et al.* 2022).

TAIWAN'S ELECTORAL SYSTEM

Election season is an exhilarating time to visit Taiwan. From main streets to back alleys, everything and everywhere is covered with election advertisements for candidates and parties. Taiwanese election campaigns contribute greatly to the vibrancy and participatory nature of Taiwanese democracy. Candidates employ the full range of campaign techniques from traditional hustings and roaming sound trucks to television advertising (including attack ads) and stadium rallies. The two main parties, and indeed some smaller parties, are highly institutionalized and well resourced. National election campaigns in particular are keenly contested and generate intense media and public interest around the world.

Elections in Taiwan are held for public office at the national (president/vice-president and the Legislative Yuan) and local level (mayors and councillors at the municipal, county and township levels). All elected officials serve four-year terms. Since the electoral system was streamlined in 2012, presidential and legislative elections are concurrently and all local electoral offices are contested at the mid-point between national elections. Direct elections for the entire Legislative Yuan and the presidency were first held in 1992 and 1996 respectively, and these "firsts" constitute consequential markers in Taiwan's progress towards democracy.

The president is elected by a first-past-the-post (FPTP) system, where the winner is decided by simple majority. These electoral rules typically produce two competitive candidates.[2] However, in 2000, Chen Shui-bian was elected president with just 39 per cent of the vote because Lian Zhan and James Soong split the KMT side of the vote. Taiwan's main legislative body is housed in the Legislative Yuan (LY). Since the 2008 election, the LY has been composed of 113 members. It was previously double in size, with smaller districts leading to the election of legislators of dubious quality, including reputed organized crime bosses. Legislators are now elected on the basis of both FPTP and proportional representation (PR). Seventy-three LY members are elected by FPTP in single member districts and a further 34 are decided by party list. This means that in addition to choosing a candidate running in their district, Taiwanese voters can indicate the party they most closely identify with or support. Regardless of who is running in their district election or for president, Taiwanese can indicate support for any political party, which enables representation by smaller parties. The probability of a small party candidate beating a DPP or KMT competitor head to head in a FPTP district election is generally low, but the party may still secure enough votes via the party list to grant them representation in the LY.

A further six seats in the LY are reserved for Indigenous legislators, who can still be members of a political party, but are elected separately. This well-intentioned reform guarantees Indigenous representation and participation, but it is an imperfect system. Indigenous representatives are voted on by all Indigenous people regardless of where in Taiwan they live, which Indigenous nation they belong to, or what languages they speak. This has led to Indigenous groups with diverse needs and agendas failing to create a strong, solidified voting bloc because of how spread

---

2. In political science, this phenomenon is referred to as "Duverger's law" (see Riker 1982).

apart different voting blocs are from each other. Although representation is meaningful, Indigenous policy has historically been modest because of how difficult it has been for Indigenous politicians to collectively push for indigenous-focused reform (Templeman 2018).

An appreciation of how Taiwan's electoral system functions is fundamental to evaluating and analysing a major election. When Taiwanese go to vote, they vote three times: first for the president, then for their local district representative, and then finally for the party they support the most. The results of the 2020 presidential race were that the DPP's incumbent president Tsai Ing-wen beat KMT candidate Han Kuo-yu and PFP candidate James Soong. Tsai won with 8,170,231 votes to Han's 5,522,119, and Song's 608,590. This represented a substantial victory for Tsai and the DPP, and a clear rejection of Han as a presidential candidate. For district votes in the LY races, the DPP won 61 seats to the KMT's 38, with small parties claiming the remaining few. This shows that in a head-to-head competition, the DPP was able to beat the KMT in more single-member districts.

But when examining the party list vote, the DPP received 33.9 per cent of the votes, the KMT 33.3 per cent of the votes, and small parties the remaining 32.7 per cent. Essentially, this is a tie between the DPP, KMT and the smaller parties. This distribution of the party vote reveals much about Taiwanese voter preferences. Even though the DPP wins more often in FPTP votes, the DPP and KMT have a similar level of base supporters who vote for these parties across the board. The KMT's party vote shows it still possesses electoral appeal, even if the party lost both the presidency and more district races than the DPP. Yet, the DPP is in a stronger position overall, since the remaining third of votes that went to small parties tend to go to the DPP in one-on-one elections. This is because more electorally viable small parties tend to be located on the DPP side of the political spectrum.

Finally, the performance of small parties shows that there is an appetite among Taiwanese voters for party choices that go beyond the centrist DPP and KMT. Third parties play an important role because they are able to put forward stronger stances on a range of issues than the major parties. Although third-party success has varied over time, they continue to win small but meaningful victories, primarily through the party list vote for the Legislature. While the two main parties, the DPP and KMT, have dominated most elections in the democratic era, Taiwan is a multi-party democracy, with over 200 parties registering with the ministry of the interior in this period. Many of these have been irrelevant or have quickly gone defunct, but others have had a meaningful impact on elections, politics and policy. For instance, the pro-unification Chinese New Party and pro-independence Taiwan Solidarity Union (led by ex-President Lee Teng-hui) had significant impact in the 1990s and 2000s, operating as parties with their more radical positions than the centrist KMT and DPP. The People First Party, a vehicle for charismatic former KMT politician James Soong, was a major player in the 2000s.

Currently, the New Power Party and Taiwan Statebuilding Party operate as explicitly pro-independence small parties. Unlike the DPP, which has managed to find a way to advocate for Taiwanese sovereignty without crossing into pro-independence, these parties openly advocate for a hypothetical Republic of Taiwan to replace the ROC. Although they maintain a more fringe position, these parties are able to win some political support during elections, often from erstwhile DPP supporters frustrated with that party's move to the centre. Another notable small party is the Taiwan People's Party, a vehicle for founder and former Taipei mayor Ko Wen-je. The party, like Ko, has an ambiguous and shifting position. As an independent (meaning he was for a long time without a political party affiliation) Ko has at various times in his career wooed the DPP, KMT and CCP, and spoken sympathetically about both independence and unification.

LOCAL ELECTIONS

Local elections are also conducted every four years, two years apart from presidential elections, and have been described as "midterm elections". However, local contests tend to have little to do with national-level politics. During local elections, mayors, county magistrates and city councillors are elected. Mayor and county magistrates are elected by FPTP voting, and the rules and outcomes are similar to that of the president and district votes. Typically only two candidates run, one each from the DPP and KMT. If a third party or independent candidate does decide to run, it will likely complicate or even spoil the race for the DPP or KMT.

City councillors are elected through a single non-transferable vote (SNTV) system. Each city council is made up of different neighbourhood representatives. Each neighbourhood has a designated number of seats in each city council. The candidates who win the most votes will win the seats in the neighbourhood. For example, if a neighbourhood has 10 seats and 20 people run, those with the top 10 most votes will win a seat. Voters only get to pick one candidate to vote for. This leads to a complex calculus in which parties must decide, based on who is popular in which neighbourhood, how many candidates from their party to field in each district, and how to spread their candidates across local councils.

The issue of cross-Strait relations is largely inconsequential for local elections, but the role of identity and party affiliation are still fundamental. Although local elections are less about national security and PRC threats, discourse about the domestic direction of Taiwan and which political party ought to lead Taiwan are salient. Identity issues still matter during local elections, but in a different way than during national elections.

A final issue to note, especially in the context of local elections, is the way in which votes are mobilized and benefits distributed. Taiwan has waged a long battle against corrupt electoral practices, which in the past have included widespread vote buying and other distorting practices. Corruption in national politics peaked during the Lee Teng-hui era, a time when *"heijin"* (black gold) described a toxic politics–business–crime nexus that corrupted politics at all levels (Chin 2003). During the past two decades, successive legislative and legal reforms (including halving the size of the Legislature) have made significant strides in eliminating overt forms of electoral fraud, such as vote buying and intimidation. Suspected or recognized organized crime leaders are no longer electorally viable in the way that they once were. And in an era of external influence in democratic elections, Taiwan's low-tech approach to registering voters and counting votes is a lesson in transparency and efficiency. However, traditional mobilizational practices with deep-seated cultural roots have not been eradicated at the local level, and vote brokers, precinct captains and influential figures in local business continue to operate on the fringes (Rich & Sullivan 2016). However, Taiwan's electoral and political system has helped Taiwan become recognized as one of the strongest democracies in Asia and globally (Papada *et al.* 2023).

THE ROLE OF TAIWANESE IDENTITY

The rise of a specifically Taiwanese identity can be traced back to the 1920s, when the Japanese colonial regime forced questions of identity and belonging onto residents. However, neither Japanese colonialism nor KMT authoritarianism allowed Taiwanese people to openly identify with or express their Taiwanese identity. It was not until democratization that identifying as Taiwanese became permissible and normalized. Routine polls have been carried out over the past three decades in an attempt to measure how Taiwanese people identify given the choice of Taiwanese, Chinese, or a combination of Taiwanese and Chinese. Again, National Chengchi University Election Study Center has the longest ongoing survey asking these questions. The results are shown in Figure 3.2.[3]

Today, just under two-thirds of people in Taiwan identify as exclusively Taiwanese. About one-third identify as both Taiwanese and Chinese. Only 2.4 per cent identify as Chinese. Over the duration of the survey, an exclusive Taiwanese identity has been growing almost monotonically, irrespective of which political party was in power.

What does it mean for someone to identify as Taiwanese, or Chinese, or both? These are conceptually and substantively complex questions (Chang & Holt 2007). But there are a few important points to consider: first, identity is one of the most important factors for everyone in Taiwan. Although identity politics matter to some extent in every country, it carries particular meaning in Taiwan because of the relationship between the political spectrum and questions of the nation's current and future identity (Chu 2004). Sometimes it is easy to differentiate when an identity is either cultural or political in nature, but questions of a Taiwanese versus Chinese identity can often be intertwined. For some respondents, identifying as Taiwanese is a national identity and separate from questions of culture. For others, Taiwanese identity is both a national and cultural identity with actors such as age and class playing important roles.

Second, what it means to be Taiwanese and Chinese can change over time and is subject to individual interpretation. Whether this

---

3. See, https://esc.nccu.edu.tw/PageDoc/Detail?fid=7800&id=6961.

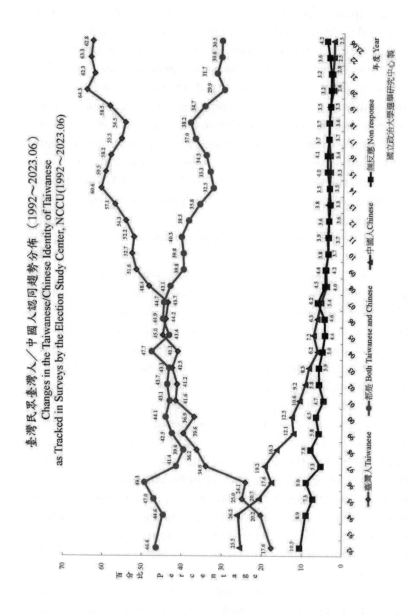

Figure 3.2 National identity preferences over time

Source: Election Study Center, National Chengchi University

identification is political, cultural, something else or a combination thereof varies according to individual subjectivity. For some, rejecting Chinese identity is a rejection of the PRC as a political system, not Chineseness as a cultural or ethnic identity (Huang 2005). Recent public opinion surveys show that many people who identify as Taiwanese still identify with Chinese culture, even though they overwhelmingly reject the PRC as a political system (Rigger *et al.* 2022).

Finally, how one identifies, as Taiwanese, Chinese, or both, does not necessarily overlay preferences for Taiwan's future national status. So much so that the substantial and growing proportion of exclusive Taiwanese identifiers has not translated into a commensurate preference for Taiwan independence. However, it does provide a clue about how the majority of people, who say they prefer the status quo, understand it, namely as de facto independence. This would also explain why both main political parties converged on this position.

This ultimately reveals one of the most difficult aspects of Taiwan's contested status. Although relatively few Taiwanese people identify as Chinese, let alone identify with the PRC, all Taiwanese people have to make political decisions with China's contested claims in mind. Taiwan's political direction is decided by the Taiwanese people, but China's continued threats against it change the way Taiwanese people think about their future. Most Taiwanese pragmatically support options that will allow them to continue enjoying a democratic and peaceful existence, even if their ideal preference might be for something else. Public opinion polling on the question of whether people would support independence if there was hypothetically no threat of a Chinese military response reveals a much higher level of latent support for independence (Hsieh & Niou 2005). Such polls show that many more Taiwanese people would choose to pursue formal independence if it were not for the PRC's intractable opposition. From the PRC's perspective, maintaining a highly credible military threat has been an effective strategy, and thus one it will likely persist with.

The trajectory of national identity opinion polling is fairly consistent over time. However, two major political events in the past decade are associated with significant spikes in identification as Taiwanese. These spikes coincide with the Sunflower Movement in 2014 and the 2019 protests and subsequent crackdown in Hong Kong.

THE SUNFLOWER MOVEMENT

In 2014, the KMT negotiated a trade bill with their counterparts in the PRC called the Cross-Strait Service Trade Agreement (CSSTA). This bill was controversial for two reasons: first, because it was negotiated behind closed doors by representative organizations on behalf of both the KMT and CCP and met in Shanghai, not Taipei. The bill was perceived to give the PRC a disproportionate degree of control over Taiwan's service sector, which in 2014 made up 70 per cent of Taiwan's GDP. The second controversy was related to how the bill was passed in Taiwan's Legislative Yuan. The KMT skipped the formal line-by-line review and passed the bill so fast that it was referred to as the "30 Second Incident".

Activists saw the KMT's actions as anti-democratic and prioritizing relations with the CCP over Taiwan's democratic institutions. Together, the lack of transparency surrounding the writing of the bill, the contents of the bill, and the way the bill was passed catalyzed a response from civil society that no one had anticipated. Beginning on 18 March, activists began what was known as the Sunflower Movement (Ho 2015). On that first night activists began to surround the Legislative Yuan building. Some broke into the parliament and began a full-fledged occupation of the building. For almost three weeks, the protesters occupied the entire neighbourhood around the Legislative Yuan, turning it into a small protest city. The protests ended on 10 April when representatives from both the DPP and KMT told protesters that the CSSTA would be shelved, withdrawn from negotiations, and never passed.

The importance of the Sunflower Movement cannot be overstated. It was a watershed moment in Taiwanese politics that served as a political awakening for young Taiwanese (Rowen 2015). The result of the protests can still be felt today with dozens of young legislators in Taiwan earning their political reputation from the Sunflower Movement. New political parties like the New Power Party and Social Democratic Party were also formed out of the movement, some of which have found electoral success in both district races and the party list (Nachman 2021). Finally, the numbers of people who identified as exclusively Taiwanese rose as a result of the movement.

The outcomes from the Sunflower Movement are more than just the trade bill's failure to pass. Protesters were not just opposed to the

CSSTA, but explicitly anti-KMT, anti-unification and pro-Taiwanese self-determination. The protesters demanded that the bill be withdrawn and that formal mechanisms be put in place to prevent similarly anti-democratic moves occurring in the future. These included more access for citizen participation in the political process. For many observers, the protest movement signalled a wake-up call, whereby average Taiwanese citizens began to feel their Taiwanese identity more strongly and believed that they ought to advocate more firmly for Taiwanese autonomy in the world.

The protests were also an important reminder that cross-Strait economics are inseparable from cross-Strait politics. Although increased trade with China would increase Taiwan's GDP, especially benefitting the many Taiwanese business interests that have invested in China's economy, it is perceived by many to be a political act that risks Taiwan's democracy and autonomy. The lack of discourse on economics or trade policy during major presidential elections in Taiwan is not because Taiwanese do not care about economic growth. It is because the issue of economic growth is deeply tied to questions of Taiwan's relationship with China, the US, and what Taiwanese people believe is the best path forward for Taiwan's future.

THE 2019 HONG KONG PROTESTS

Hong Kong is of special interest to Taiwanese people, who observe developments there keenly. Hong Kong returned to PRC rule in 1997 under the auspices of "one country, two systems", a framework that promised Hong Kong limited but meaningful democratic autonomy. Since Hong Kong's handover to the PRC, Taiwan has closely observed how such political systems set in place by the PRC work in practice. In 2019, however, Hong Kong's system began to change, beginning with the introduction of an extradition bill that prompted fears about the erosion of Hong Kong's remaining freedoms. The catalyst was ironically the murder of a Hong Konger in Taiwan. Since there was no extradition treaty with Taiwan because of its contested status, the Hong Kong executive introduced a new, far-reaching bill that would have allowed anyone residing in Hong Kong to be extradited to Beijing at the PRC government's request. It prompted an immediate backlash from academics, lawyers, politicians and human rights organizations. This evolved into a watershed social protest movement that continued for nearly two years until the Covid-19 pandemic. Ultimately, the central government in Beijing decided that this challenge to authority and widespread social instability required intercession. In July 2020, a new Hong Kong National Security Law was passed by the PRC government, with such far-reaching consequences that many analysts feared the end of "one country, two systems" and the beginning of a new authoritarian regime in Hong Kong (Chan *et al.* 2020).

Taiwan watched closely throughout the entire life cycle of the Hong Kong protests, which became a salient issue during Taiwan's 2020 presidential and legislative elections. Every politician from the major parties felt obliged to endorse the Hong Kong protesters and stand with their cause for democracy. For the DPP in particular, this became the dominant lens through which they filtered their campaign rhetoric. Demonstrations convened in solidarity with Hong Kongers were held across Taiwan throughout the duration of the protests. The slogan, "Today Hong Kong, Tomorrow Taiwan", first heard during the Sunflower Movement, was highly noticeable. It encapsulated warnings about "one country, two systems", the trustworthiness of the CCP and the Chinese government, just as Tsai's KMT opponent in the election, Han Kuo-yu, was proposing pro-China engagement policies. Tsai won the election handily, and Hong Kong was certainly a factor.

In the rhetorical and symbolic terms of an election campaign, Taiwanese politicians largely stood in solidarity with the Hong Kong protestors. Substantively, however, support has varied, and after the conclusion of the election campaign public opinion has indicated mixed feelings about Hong Kong. Hong Kongers themselves indicated that if they were to flee Hong Kong, Taiwan would be among their first-choice destinations (Nachman *et al.* 2020), but not all Taiwanese warmed to the prospect of a wave of incoming migrants. Opinion surveys show a majority of Taiwanese support the Hong Kong protests, while approval of policies to help Hong Kongers was significantly lower (Nachman *et al.* 2021). The Taiwanese government's strong rhetorical support was accompanied by minor institutional changes and selective help for Hong Kongers with wealth or tech-industry skills. Vulnerable protesters who needed refuge and sought out Taiwan ended up becoming a far more politically sensitive issue and were often turned away. The Taiwanese government was only able to offer limited help, largely because of Taiwan's lack of a refugee law (Hioe & Nachman 2019). Without legislation, there were no standard practices or regulations for how to deal with Hong Konger's needing immediate humanitarian assistance from the Taiwanese government. Hundreds of Hong Kongers were still able to flee to Taiwan, but their journeys have been difficult despite initial good intentions from Taiwan (Tsao 2020).

OTHER SALIENT ISSUES IN TAIWANESE POLITICS

Many issues that are ostensibly unrelated to national identity or cross-Strait relations tend to be filtered through the lens of Taiwan's status and future. During national elections, candidates spend most of their time talking about how they will safeguard Taiwan, lead Taiwan to a better future, or other broad promises about national security (Sullivan 2008). Policy issues on the economy, the environment, or social change are typically relegated to the background. This does not mean that citizens do not also demand these kinds of changes, but during presidential elections citizens are more concerned about whether or not the next president is going to align Taiwan more closely with China or not (Fell 2006).

Non-election years are typically the time for civil society and politicians to try to push for policy changes that are neglected during the national election cycle, such as wages and labour practices, which are in dire need of reform but are almost never discussed during major elections. They tend to be left to the years in between elections to be resolved.

After sketching out the preferences of Taiwanese voters in this chapter, it should be clear that identity and concerns and ambitions for Taiwan's future status define politics in ways that are distinct from most other democracies. Although these are critical questions for Taiwanese politicians and voters, because of Taiwan's contested status they are also crucial to the two outside actors with a special interest in Taiwan, the PRC and the US. We deal with the most important of these actors first, the PRC, which claims Taiwan as its own.

4

Taiwan and the ROC

The seemingly facile question of what to call Taiwan is politically sensitive and hotly contested. Strictly speaking, "Taiwan" is a geographical term referring to the largest of four islands under the jurisdiction of the ROC – Taiwan, Kinmen, Penghu and Matsu.[1] But where does seeing Taiwan as a geographic location and the ROC as a contested state begin to blur? What is the difference between Taiwan and the ROC? Although some observers imply that ROC is merely Taiwan's "formal name" it is more complicated than that. Indeed, Taiwan's relationship to the ROC is not straightforward. The continued existence of the ROC is crucial to understanding Taiwan's international situation, its relations with the PRC and Taiwanese domestic political competition. Empirically speaking, the ROC is a discrete, functionally autonomous, liberal democratic polity that is de facto independent. The ROC has its own distinct political system, currency and military. It raises its own taxes and conducts its own foreign policy, albeit within parameters that are affected by its disputed status. The ROC cannot participate in international organizations for which statehood is a membership criteria, and the PRC even attempts to influence what Taiwan can do informally.

THE ROC–KMT CONNECTION

The KMT has its roots in organizations formed as the Qing dynasty collapsed and revolutionaries like Sun Yat-sen put forward alternatives

---

1. Kinmen is also spelled Jinmen, while Matsu can be rendered Mazu. The islands of Penghu are sometimes referred to in English as the Pescadores.

for China's future. The KMT evolved out of two revolutionary groups founded by Sun, the Revive China Society (*Xing Zhong Hui*, founded in Hawaii in 1894) and the United League (*Tong Meng Hui*, founded in Tokyo in 1905), as vehicles for overthrowing a Qing government besieged by imperial aggressors, domestic rebellion and internal dysfunction.

Following the conclusion of the Xinhai Revolution that ended dynastic China in 1911, Sun became the first (temporary) leader of the ROC. Sun also went on to oversee the foundation of the KMT, the Chinese Nationalist Party to give it its full name, in 1919. After Sun's death in 1925, Chiang Kai-shek assumed leadership of the KMT and reunified a country fragmented by warlordism under the leadership of his Nationalist government. The ROC and KMT have always been intimately connected, and the legacy of this connection created complexities many decades later in Taiwan.

When Japan invaded China in the 1930s, Chiang led the resistance, in concert with the Communists. Following Japan's defeat in the Second World War, Chiang's Nationalists and Mao's Communists resumed their long conflict that the common Japanese enemy had temporarily suspended. By 1947 the Nationalist army was suffering unsustainable losses, kickstarting a two-year mass evacuation of officials, soldiers and supporters to the island of Taiwan. In 1949, as Mao led the establishment of the PRC, Chiang and his KMT government set up in exile in Taiwan.

The ROC constitution and political system were fully reproduced in Taiwan, including the five branches of government, the operation of the military and judiciary, and the various elements of the ROC's political culture. The latter included Sun Yat-sen's political philosophy encapsulated in his "Three Principles of the People".[2] As "father of the nation" Sun's portrait still adorns government buildings and other symbols of state in Taiwan. Indeed, memorial buildings and parks commemorating Sun occupy prime real estate in both the ROC (Taipei) and PRC (Guangzhou).

Exiled to Taiwan, under Chiang Kai-shek the ROC's political and cultural imagination was rooted in loss and longing for the Chinese

2. Sun's Three Principles are nationalism, democracy and people's livelihood. They form part of his blueprint for the reconstruction of a stronger and fairer China as developed in his treatise, *Fundamentals of National Reconstruction* (1923).

homeland. Chiang's KMT regime saw itself as the true representative and defender of the "real China", contrary to what they decried as an illegitimate communist usurper in Beijing. The KMT maintained all the customs and appendages of the "original ROC" that had ruled in China from 1912 to 1949. Media and popular culture were infused with traditional Chinese elements and nostalgia. For decades, geography, history and literature classes in schools at all levels taught only about China and barely mentioned Taiwan. Taiwan's streets were named after Chinese geographical features, classical Chinese culture and Chiang's political ambitions, such as "restoration". ROC parliamentary bodies retained seats for representatives of provinces now located in the PRC. The removal of these superfluous and underemployed representatives was a major point of contention for opposition activists. The eventual reform of the legislature and redundancy for these "old thieves" was a symbolic moment in Taiwan's democratization.

The transition from authoritarian regime to consolidated democracy was full of struggles over language, history, symbols and naming conventions. For example, it was not until the Chen Shui-bian administrations (2000–08) that textbooks and curricula were revised to focus more on Taiwan and less on China. Much progress has been made in terms of recentring Taiwan in the national curriculum, in media and cultural products. But symbols and practical features of the KMT regime are everywhere. Chiang Kai-shek's memorial was renamed Liberty Square and dozens of Chiang statues have been removed, but the quotidian reminders of the *ancien régime* are ubiquitous even now – the system of government, the public holidays, images on the currency, and the continued viability of the KMT as one of Taiwan's two main political parties. Several hundred streets are still named after Sun Yat-sen and Chiang Kai-shek. Most fundamentally, the ROC constitution remains the law of the land, and rewriting or even amending the constitution is a political battleground in Taiwan and a red line for the PRC, which sees it as a precursor of Taiwan independence.

The connection between the KMT and the ROC remains in effect today, albeit in reduced intensity and scale to the Chiang era. After decades of "exile" in Taiwan, it became evident that the KMT would never lead the ROC to "retake" China. Most *waishengren* came to accept Taiwan as their home due to the passage of time, intermarriage with *benshengren*, and generations born in Taiwan who knew of China only from books and film. When the dream of restoring the ROC to China by force receded, for a significant cohort within the KMT it was sublimated into Chinese unification under the auspices of the ROC. However, as democratization proceeded and public opinion shifted toward greater identification with Taiwan, the KMT position changed too. Notably, in 1991, the KMT government lifted the "Temporary Provisions Effective During the Period of National Mobilization for Suppression of the Communist Rebellion" (Temporary Provisions), which implicitly acknowledged the futility of the ROC's claim to rule all of China.

Recognition of this reality marked the start of a transition to (KMT) President Lee Teng-hui's informal but ostensible "Two Chinas" position. Lee's statement in 1999 that "the ROC has been a sovereign state since it was founded in 1912 [and] consequently there is no need to declare independence", provoked fury in Beijing. Lee is reviled in the PRC as a traitor to One China, even after his death in 2020. Lee's argument strongly influenced Taiwan's attitude to its existing and possible future status. The mainstreams of both main parties converged on Lee's position in subsequent decades. The key for many KMT officials and supporters remains the preservation and continuation of the ROC, and retention of the ROC's Chinese cultural legacy for Taiwan. Although there is a small cohort of die-hard unification supporters within the KMT, it is more accurate to describe the KMT as a pro-ROC than a pro-unification party (Drun 2021).

The baggage of the ROC's authoritarian past remains a contemporary issue for the KMT, particularly its inability or reluctance to commit to a Taiwan-centred future. While the DPP acknowledges the existence of a Taiwanese nation, and accepts that pursuit of it comes with a price, in terms of threats from the PRC, the KMT resists the idea. Indeed, there is a current within the KMT that insists not just on the preservation of the ROC, but the "restoration" of a traditional vision of the ROC, including resistance to cultural localization, an emphasis on Taiwan's Chinese cultural heritage and openness to engagement with China in the form of the PRC.

In the following sections we discuss three issues pertaining to Taiwan's relationship to the ROC from the perspective of three different ROC presidents, Chen Shui-bian, Ma Ying-jeou and Tsai Ing-wen. The preferences and programmes of presidents, two from the DPP and one from the KMT, illuminate distinct aspects of Taiwanese party politics as it pertains to key issues such as One China, "independence" and the nature of relations with the PRC.

CHEN SHUI-BIAN (2000–08), THE DPP AND "TAIWAN INDEPENDENCE"

The DPP has long been depicted, by the PRC, international observers and a portion of the Taiwanese electorate, as an "independence party". We interpret "independence party" to imply that the DPP is an advocate for a formal declaration of *de jure* independence. Chen's Taiwanese nationalism and nation-building efforts represented a significant break from decades of ROC-centric KMT rule, and conventional wisdom of the time implied this constituted "Taiwan independence". In Beijing and Washington the "pro-independence" label was a pejorative, since it meant the pursuit of something inherently dangerous and destabilizing. Among Taiwanese voters it could be a liability too, for similar reasons. However, the DPP's position with regard to independence is more nuanced and far from unanimous. The presidency of Chen Shui-bian, the first ROC president to come from the DPP, marked a high (or low) point for associations between the DPP and "Taiwan independence" (Sullivan & Lowe 2010). Perceptions of Chen as an advocate for "Taiwan independence" caused his tenure to be marked by fractious relations with the PRC and the US, and created significant domestic divisions.

The call for an independent Taiwan became a rallying call for some *benshengren* activists in the 1960s and 1970s. Advocacy of independence during the martial law era was punishable by the state, sometimes brutally. Underground independence activists introduced an idea that was unthinkable under the KMT: a hypothetical "Republic of Taiwan" that would be independent of *both* the PRC and the KMT-led ROC. Only then, proponents argued, would Taiwan's decolonization be truly complete. Taiwan independence was advocated by some in the DPP when it formed in 1986, in part as a way of cohering a loose organization made up of diverse and divisive factions. The DPP's position on Taiwan independence was concretized in 1991 when "independence by plebiscite" was written into the party platform. Although it suited some of the DPP's core support, the explicit pursuit of formal independence was not just a suboptimal electoral strategy, it was a liability. Mainstream public opinion did not favour "Taiwan independence", and DPP election candidates were vulnerable to KMT messaging that a vote for the DPP equalled a vote for war with the PRC.

After years of intense intra-party debate, the DPP announced at its party assembly meeting in 1999 a consequential new position. The party's Resolution on Taiwan's Future stated that "Taiwan is a sovereign and independent country [...] named the Republic of China under its current constitution" (DPP 1999). The formal ambition of "independence by plebiscite" was replaced by the more neutral demand that any changes in the status quo "must be decided by all the residents of Taiwan by means of plebiscite". The resolution represented the DPP's acceptance of the ROC, albeit grudging and as an expedient. It also represented a convergence between the DPP position and the one expressed by Lee Teng-hui in the final years of his tenure, namely Taiwanese self-determination within the status quo framework of ROC sovereignty.

The DPP's decision to give up the formal pursuit of "Taiwan independence" was far from unanimously supported by the party membership, leading to schisms and even splinter parties breaking away. However, it was beneficial for the DPP's electoral fortunes. The DPP's credibility at the polls was enhanced to the extent that four years after the disastrous failure of Peng Ming-min's run for president in 1996 on an explicit "Taiwan independence" platform, Chen Shui-bian won election. Chen's campaign was notable for its moderation and avoidance of "Taiwan independence" (Fell 2006), although his victory (with 37 per cent of the vote) was only possible because the KMT vote was split between two competing candidates.

The "overarching consensus" that emerged in Taiwanese politics at the turn of the century was that the ROC was an independent sovereign entity (Schubert 2004). For the DPP, the pursuit of "Taiwan independence" remained a potential future option but not a necessity, since Taiwan was already independent under the ROC. For the PRC, it created two challenges. First, KMT–DPP convergence on the existing independence of the ROC challenged the One-China principle by suggesting that there were "Two Chinas". Second, rejecting "Taiwan independence" created political space for the DPP during Chen's presidency to pursue a concerted programme of localization. This effectively replaced the former emphasis on Taiwan's "Chineseness" in favour of "Taiwaneseness". The PRC decried Chen's many efforts to reform cultural institutions, the education curriculum, and replace Chinese names and symbols, as de-Sinicization. Chen actively emphasized a specific Taiwanese national identity, democratic consolidation and cultural localization to consolidate Taiwan's distinctiveness and separation from the PRC. Taiwan-centred identities became normalized in official discourse and were reflected in changes in public opinion during the Chen era (Zhong 2016). But did Chen's efforts constitute "Taiwan independence"?

Chen's policy on independence for seven of his eight years as president was defined by the "Four Nos". As long as China did not attack Taiwan, Chen's policy was that he and the DPP *would not* declare independence, change the name of the ROC, change the ROC constitution, or push for a public referendum over the question of independence. Contrary to the perception that he was advocating for independence, his policy initiatives stated otherwise.

Yet, from the PRC perspective, Chen's rhetoric frequently contravened the One-China principle. For instance, in 2003 he stated that "the Republic of China is a sovereign state. This is the clear and obvious status of our country. The ROC effectively exercises jurisdiction over the islands of Taiwan, Penghu, Jinmen and Mazu – a fact no one can deny" (Li *et al.* 2009: 378). And Chen's concrete actions such as legislating for referendums, seeking to join the UN, and replacing "ROC" with "Taiwan" on passports were interpreted by the PRC as signals of incremental moves toward independence. Yet, there was no real possibility that Chen would try to declare "Taiwan independence". Operating for much of his tenure under conditions of divided government and an ROC constitution that does not provide the president with such unilateral powers, Chen had neither the power nor mechanisms to declare independence. Furthermore, the US and other international actors aside from the PRC, were clear in their opposition to Chen's signalling and policy initiatives. Nonetheless, Chen's dominance of the rhetorical arena and propensity for making bald statements shorn of any diplomatic finesse, earned him international notoriety and criticism for his reckless "revisionism" and pursuit of "Taiwan independence" (Ross 2006).

Chen had once been a proponent of "Taiwan independence", declaring publicly as an aspiring politician many years earlier "long live Taiwan independence!" However, Chen, like the DPP, had moved toward the centre and majority public opinion, as evidenced by his studied moderation on the issue during the 2000 presidential election campaign. As a political goal, "Taiwan independence" had by then become "so marginalised that overt promotion of independence within the political arena has all but disappeared" (Rigger 2001: 104). Endorsement of "Taiwan independence" was "electoral poison" and mainstream Taiwanese politicians (and voters) generally accepted that reality (Fell 2005: 122).

Chen remains an ambivalent figure in Taiwanese politics. His period in power was punctuated by governance failings and bitter partisanship. Stymied by an obstructionist opposition controlling the legislature, and ignored by the PRC, Chen turned increasingly to stoking Taiwanese nationalism. In 2007, in the midst of major political scandals for the president and his party, Chen relaunched his "Four Nos" policy as the "Four Wants", namely "Taiwan wants independence, Taiwan wants to change its name, Taiwan wants a new constitution, and Taiwan wants development". This radical switch from a pragmatic policy to an overtly provocative one while mired in corruption scandals hurt his legacy and, for many years afterwards, the DPP's electability. At the end of an exhausting and divisive second term, Chen was convicted on serious corruption charges. Subsequently jailed and in failing health, Chen's demise does not detract from the significant influence he had on Taiwan's political development.

MA YING-JEOU (2008–16) AND THE "1992 CONSENSUS"

Ma Ying-jeou's tenure as ROC president was characterized by an anomalous period of cross-Strait cooperation and goodwill. Ma's emphasis on the Chinese heritage of the ROC reflected his commitment to the ROC and an understanding of the ROC's relationship to Taiwan and the PRC that was very different from Chen. His willingness to acknowledge the concept of One China assuaged PRC concerns about Taiwan's direction of travel after Chen, but Ma's unwillingness or inability to advance the PRC's unification cause was ultimately a disappointment. Within Taiwan, Ma's detente policies toward the PRC and foregrounding of the

ROC to the detriment of a Taiwan-centric programme, led to a significant popular backlash.

A former personal secretary to Chiang Ching-kuo, Ma was steeped
in KMT politics and reverence for the ROC, despite earlier in his career
cultivating a "local image" by learning local languages and making
appeals to Taiwanese identity in his election campaigns. As president
he emphasized the Chinese aspects of Taiwan's historical and cultural
heritage and pushed for restoring the centrality of Chinese identity to
Taiwan. His identification with Chineseness and the idea of an essentially
Chinese nation located in Taiwan represented a major shift away from
localizing trends in politics and society. Ma's references to the mythical
Yan and Yellow Emperors were incongruous to most Taiwanese. In its
fixation on restoring a traditional version of the ROC with its emphasis on Chinese culture and heritage, the KMT had found it challenging
to present a Taiwan-centred vision that was compatible with trends in
national identity. Post-Ma, the party has continued to struggle to connect with younger people, for whom China has little connection to their
lived reality as Taiwanese.

Ma's rejection of cultural localization indirectly assuaged PRC concerns about Taiwan consolidating its distinctiveness and separation
under Chen. He also addressed them directly, immediately committing
to the idea of One China. He did so by endorsing the "1992 Consensus",
the conceit that there is only One China but the ROC and PRC have
their "respective interpretations" about which government is the legitimate representative of it. The 1992 Consensus is a piece of diplomatic
finesse relating to an informal meeting between CCP and KMT representatives in Hong Kong in 1992 and coined a decade later by a KMT
official. There was never a formal document signed or shared, and it
is uncertain whether any such "consensus" existed. Moreover, there are
serious doubts, emphasized by the DPP, about the relevance of a "consensus" reached by a then-unelected KMT and an authoritarian CCP for
contemporary democratic Taiwan. More damaging still for Taiwanese
proponents of the 1992 Consensus is that the PRC and Xi Jinping himself have explicitly stated that they do not accept the "respective interpretations" qualifier.

Ma was willing to overlook these serious challenges to the integrity
of the 1992 Consensus because it created space for the ROC to exist and

held out the promise of more stable cross-Strait relations. In fact, Ma's embrace of the 1992 Consensus proved it to be a very useful construction, as cross-Strait relations under Ma were extraordinary for the extent of bilateral cooperation. Building on several years of informal communications between the KMT and CCP, the two sides agreed to a "diplomatic truce", discontinuing the unseemly competition for diplomatic allies. The PRC agreed to limited participation in international organizations for Taiwan, including attendance at World Health Assembly meetings that was later denied during the Covid-19 pandemic. By the end of his final term, Ma's administration had concluded 23 practical agreements across multiple sectors and facilitated party-to-party talks that led to the first ever meeting of sitting PRC and ROC presidents in Singapore in November 2015.

However, Ma's positive posturing towards the PRC became increasingly unpopular at home, and in the end, his pro-China stance came at a cost. Domestically, the more he expanded relations with China the more civil society pushed back. In 2014, Ma and the KMT tried to push through an even deeper trade deal with China called the Cross-Strait Service Trade Agreement. The deal was seen as too pro-China by many Taiwanese people and gave rise to the Sunflower Movement discussed in the previous chapter (Nachman 2018). Ma and the KMT were severely damaged by the impression that these cross-Strait policies prioritized China over Taiwan.

Ma's impressive slate of cross-Strait agreements cannot mask the fact that the underlying militarization of the Strait and the direct military threat to the ROC remained unchanged. The temperature of cross-Strait relations was tepid, but the PRC's military posture represented an undiminished threat to Taiwan's national security despite Ma's overtly friendly orientation. Ma's experience illustrated the reality that no ROC president will be able to deliver what the PRC wants, i.e. a political resolution resulting in unification on the PRC's terms. For all the superficial goodwill and friendship expressed during Ma's tenure, Ma was a disappointment for Beijing. He wanted peaceful and productive cross-Strait relations and was prepared to make accommodations to secure it. Yet, for all his assurances to Beijing that he would uphold the idea of One China, Ma was not a unificationist. He was committed to the ROC. However, Ma and many of his KMT colleagues' adherence to preserving the ROC is at odds with the PRC's consistent and explicit denial of the ROC's right to exist. The KMT's argument that the ROC can coexist safely and productively with the PRC under the auspices of One China and the 1992 Consensus is increasingly untenable as PRC impatience for unification becomes more evident under Xi Jinping. The KMT sought solace in the 1992 Consensus of "One China, respective interpretations", but doing so required a wilful suspension of disbelief, since the PRC does not accept the indefinite continuation of the ROC.

TSAI ING-WEN (2016–24) AND THE STATUS QUO

"Status quo" is a key and hotly contested concept linking the political identity of Taiwan, the ROC and prospects for cross-Strait relations. It is one of the more dynamic, opaque and malleable concepts in cross-Strait politics, and the behaviours of the main actors (including Taiwanese voters) are conditioned by their interpretation of the status quo. For the PRC, the status quo is that Taiwan is an indivisible part of China's sovereign territory that is currently outside of the PRC's jurisdiction. For the PRC, this is a lamentable situation and the CCP regime is sworn to remedy it through "peaceful unification" if possible, while retaining the right to use force if not. For the US, the status quo is that the PRC and Taiwan are currently separated and that any change to that situation must be arrived at peacefully and endorsed by people on both sides, while also opposing that either side make a unilateral change. While the PRC and US see the status quo differently, their positions have been relatively stable for decades. By contrast, domestic political actors in Taiwan have actively interpreted and reinterpreted the meaning of status quo according to ideology, identity politics and their individual preferences for Taiwan's national status. Ma Ying-jeou shifted understandings of the status quo to fit the basic terms of the 1992 Consensus, namely that the ROC was imbued with sovereignty but only as part of One China. This represented a step away from the "Two Chinas" formulations favoured by Lee Teng-hui and Chen Shui-bian, but not so far as to embrace unification. Under Tsai Ing-wen, the status quo became a central concept governing Taiwan's cross-Strait policy and Taiwan's engagement with the US and broader West.

Taiwanese leaders are constrained by the politically possible in terms of the PRC's posture, domestic public opinion and international political support. Due to the threat of military action, Taiwanese leaders understand the risks involved in advocating for "Taiwan independence". While some politicians do explicitly cultivate support among the small part of the electorate that wants "Taiwan independence", most temper their positions in order to appeal to more voters. Many mainstream politicians have accepted the liminality and ambiguities of the status quo, accepting that *de jure* independence is a dead-end and instead advocating consolidation of Taiwan's de facto independence. Tsai Ing-wen's evolution as a politician reflected these dynamics. Learning from a failed presidential campaign in 2012 when her China policy came under attack from the KMT and was obliquely criticized by the US, Tsai Ing-wen's mantra since standing for president in 2016 was "maintain the status quo". She repeatedly pledged to "maintain the status quo" if elected and, after she won, continued to emphasize it while reframing what it meant conceptually and in practice. Incremental changes to how the status quo was operationalized by Taiwan and understood internationally during Tsai's tenure, demonstrated the shifting quality of the concept, and helped explain increasing PRC anxieties about Taiwan's trajectory. Tsai's fundamental understanding of the status quo was that Taiwan, in the guise of the ROC, was already an independent sovereign nation and thus another hypothetical form of "Taiwan independence" was superfluous.

If this argument sounds familiar it is because Tsai had a hand, as an advisor to former president Lee Teng-hui, in the antecedent "two state theory" position that Lee put forward in 1999. This position is not universally popular within the DPP or among supporters of "Taiwan independence", for whom the ROC remains an alien colonial regime indelibly tainted by the KMT's four-decade authoritarian rule. However, Tsai introduced some conceptual finesse, distinguishing between the ROC that ruled China from 1912 to 1949 and the "ROC on Taiwan" from 1949 to the present. While the "ROC on Taiwan" was once a repressive authoritarian regime dominated by *waishengren*, democratization made self-rule by the Taiwanese people possible. In this telling, democratization was equivalent to Taiwan gaining "independence", manifest in the right of Taiwanese people to choose their leaders and exercise their democratic rights and freedoms.

Having made an argument for the necessary continuation of the ROC framework as the status quo, Tsai set out a forward-looking vision for Taiwan based on democratic and liberal values. In it, she foregrounded the community of diverse ethnic groups that live in Taiwan, the historical specificity and cultural hybridity that makes Taiwan distinct from both the PRC and the traditional version of the ROC. Tsai sometimes referred to this as a "Taiwan Consensus", in contradistinction to the 1992 Consensus. It is these elements of Taiwanese identity that form the basis of attempts to concretize Taiwan's distinctiveness from China. The distinction is sharpened by the PRC's hostility, including its refusal to renounce the use of force, and its aggressive efforts to coerce Taiwan into accepting PRC-authored unification under "one country, two systems".

Contrary to Ma Ying-jeou, Tsai explicitly rejected the 1992 Consensus, refusing to countenance Taiwan's potential future options being constrained by a purported agreement between two parties that were unelected by the Taiwanese people. Tsai acknowledged the "historical fact" of the 1992 Consensus, accepting that a meeting took place and views were exchanged, but rejected the content. Her rejection of One China, and refusal to feign belief in the "respective interpretations" conceit, was a challenge to the PRC's One-China principle while not constituting "Taiwan independence".

Tsai's articulation of Taiwan's status within the ROC framework was palatable for the US and other western countries because it ostensibly preserved the status quo, which has been the long-term goal of western policy toward Taiwan. The different reception that Tsai Ing-wen received two decades removed from Chen Shui-bian's ostracism for voicing similar positions, spoke to the significant changes in the international milieu and western countries' reassessment of the foreign policy ambitions and behaviours of the PRC under Xi Jinping. However, interpreted in Beijing as a form of independence by salami-slicing stealth, Tsai's interpretation of the status quo was anathema to the PRC, which has consistently rejected the possibility of an "independent ROC" outside the framework of One China. These dynamics contributed to PRC fears that Taiwan was drifting further away from unification, partly explaining the greater urgency and recent intensification of Chinese pressures exerted on Taiwan.

As intimated in this chapter, Taiwan's transition to democracy complicated Taiwan's relationship with both the ROC and PRC by opening up space for different possibilities. The freedoms and rights associated with a democratic polity created opportunities for different expressions of national identity. And democratic values became a central factor in many Taiwanese people's identification with Taiwan, and rejection of the PRC.

5

Sacred and inviolable

On the eve of the Taiwanese presidential election in 2016, Chinese cyberspace erupted in fury when footage emerged of 16-year-old Chou Tzu-yu of K-pop girl group TWICE holding a small ROC flag on a Korean television show. Chou, known by her stage name of Tzuyu, is a Taiwanese citizen, and held the ROC flag along with the other TWICE members who held flags from their own home countries. But in China, Tzuyu became an object of righteous nationalistic anger for her purported promotion of "Taiwan independence" (Buckley & Wang 2016). Accusing Tzuyu of promoting Taiwanese independence over an ROC flag is deeply ironic. She was not holding up any of the flags or symbols associated with "Taiwan independence", usually green and white, but the ROC's "blue sky, white sun and wholly red earth", something with deep Chinese resonances. Advocates of independence in Taiwan see the ROC flag as a symbol of unification and Chinese control over Taiwan and would likely never be seen flying it.

At the time, the PRC still advocated the 1992 Consensus, a concept that permitted the existence of the ROC through the notion of "One China, respective interpretations". The fact that the ROC flag could prompt such controversy, when ROC symbols within Taiwan were more likely to be associated with the KMT and openness to close relations with the PRC, is symptomatic of the confusion, complexities and sensitivities involved in cross-Strait relations. These nuances may have been lost on JYP, TWICE's record label, which was compelled by the threat of losing access to the Chinese market to film a "hostage-style" apology video. In it, an abject Tzuyu dressed in all black, affirmed the existence of One China and her undying adherence to it (Ahn & Lin 2019).

We could add dozens of other examples of Chinese anger being directed at individuals or companies whose actions were interpreted as an act of recognizing Taiwan: an American airline with Taiwan as an option on drop-down menus for online bookings (Wee 2018); a former WWE wrestler turned Hollywood actor who inadvertently implied Taiwan was a country (Victor 2021); a European state that allowed the use of "Taiwanese" to be applied to Taiwan's representative office, and so on (Lau & Momtaz 2021). Some of these reactions can be attributed to the over-exuberance of cyber-nationalist communities online, or over-zealous foreign ministry officials hoping to get noticed by their superiors by demonstrating fealty to Xi Jinping's demands for a robust foreign policy posture.

Such hypersensitivity has been widely interpreted in popular accounts as symbolizing authoritarian pathologies or overreach by an overweening party-state. The aim of this chapter is to assess the PRC's position on Taiwan and in doing so to try to show how apparently inexplicable overreactions can be understood.

ORIGINS OF THE CLAIM THAT TAIWAN IS PART OF CHINA

The PRC's position on Taiwan is that it is an inviolable part of Chinese territory and has been so since "ancient times". "Complete unification of the motherland" is a central goal of the Chinese leadership and a central component of "great rejuvenation of the Chinese nation", with a quasi-deadline of the centenary of the founding of the PRC in 2049. Unification is both a "sacred duty" and a "historic mission" for the CCP. It is also a key marker by which the legitimacy of the CCP regime is measured. The "Taiwan question" is a significant issue in Sino-US relations and the most important of the "core issues of national interest" on which the PRC pledges zero compromise and refuses to countenance outside interference.

The PRC position has been formally set out in the constitution, in domestic legislation, notably the 2005 Anti-Secession Law (Ji 2006), and in white papers published in 1993, 2000 and 2022.[1] The PRC has

---

1. The 1993 white paper is available at http://www.china.org.cn/e-white/taiwan/

reiterated it and put it on record in various communiqués issued in international and bilateral fora. Fundamental positions, such as the One-China principle (different from the US and other countries' One China *policies*), pervade all other policymaking and the PRC's foreign relations and diplomacy. It is impossible to overstate the centrality of Taiwan to the contemporary PRC, even while acknowledging the work produced by historians showing the fixation on Taiwan to be a modern phenomenon (Hayton 2020). Indeed, in the 1930s, during the Japanese colonial era in Taiwan, the CCP and Mao himself reportedly supported Taiwan's independence (Tsang 2008: 5).

The legal interpretation of Taiwan's status begins with the defeat of Japan at the end of the Second World War and the "return" of Japan's colonial possessions and occupied territories gained through aggression. At the time, the ROC under the KMT was accepted as the legitimate governing body of China. The Chinese government's declaration of war against Japan in 1941 abrogated all bilateral treaties, which included China's ceding of Taiwan to Japan in 1895. Second, the Cairo Declaration of 1943 issued by the US, UK and China (i.e. the ROC) stated that Chinese territories occupied by Japan would ultimately be returned to China (at the time, the ROC).[2] This was reiterated by the same three parties, and later the USSR, through the Potsdam Proclamation in 1945.[3] The PRC maintains that when Japan signed the instrument of surrender, Taiwan was returned to "China", i.e. not the ROC per se, but whichever government was recognized as the sovereign of China.

After the war, the ROC formally resumed the exercise of sovereignty over Taiwan. Two sources of confusion enter at this point, albeit not according to the PRC's view. First, there is some confusion about whether Japan actually "returned Taiwan to China", or merely renounced sovereignty over Taiwan. This question was not elucidated in the Treaty of

---

index.htm; the 2000 iteration at http://www.taiwandocuments.org/white.htm; and the latest version at https://english.news.cn/20220810/df9d3b8702154b34 bbf1d451b99bf64a/c.html.

2. Text available at https://digitalarchive.wilsoncenter.org/document/cairo-declaration.

3. Text available at https://www.ndl.go.jp/constitution/e/etc/c06.html#:~:text=We %2Dthe%20President%20of%20the,opportunity%20to%20end%20this%20war.

San Francisco in 1952, to which neither the ROC nor PRC were parties, which formally ended the state of war and established the foundation for US–Japan security arrangements. The pursuant Treaty of Taipei, signed by Japan and the ROC in 1952, formally ended the Sino-Japanese War and mirrored the Treaty of San Francisco in key respects, but did not explicitly address the return/renounce question. The PRC prefers not to foreground these ambiguities, insisting that Taiwan was simply returned to China.

This raises another question. Assuming Taiwan was returned to China in 1945, would that not mean it was returned to the ROC, since the PRC did not exist until 1949? On this point, the PRC argument is that as soon as the PRC was established, Chinese sovereignty was transferred from the ROC to the PRC, making the PRC the legitimate ruler of all Chinese territories, including Taiwan. Since it is now universally recognized that the PRC holds legitimate sovereignty over Chinese territory, the PRC argues that if Taiwan was returned to China it must mean that Taiwan is legitimately part of the PRC. The PRC argues that when the PRC was founded it became the successor to the ROC (a new dynasty in effect) and subsequently became the embodiment of One China. Another complication enters at this point: despite PRC claims to the contrary, the ROC did not simply cease to exist after 1949. It carried on as a viable and empirically observed entity on Taiwan. Furthermore, it did so while meeting all of the criteria by which the definition of statehood is measured, and for several decades was widely recognized as such (Shen 1999).

That changed with the gradual shift in recognition towards the PRC and away from the ROC that culminated in the normalization of diplomatic relations between the US and PRC in the 1970s. This diplomatic watershed precipitated a widespread switch of diplomatic recognition from the ROC to the PRC, continuing over the following decades to the point where the ROC is currently recognized by just 12 states and the Vatican. This development does not change the reality that the ROC continues to be a viable entity restricted to Taiwan, nor the fact that Taiwan under the ROC framework became a global economic and technology power and beacon of democracy in Asia. The PRC was encouraged by the growing global recognition of the PRC as the "sole legal government of China", and by widespread *acknowledgement* of its claims to Taiwan. However, to the PRC's chagrin and increasing frustration, it was not accompanied by, nor did it lead to, mass *recognition* of the PRC's claim to sovereignty over Taiwan.

China's claims over Taiwan range from essentialist historical arguments to interpretations of different treaties and diplomatic peace-time agreements. Because so many of these formal documents and diplomatic statements are steeped in vague wording, it has allowed claims to Taiwan to be interpreted differently by various parties to fit their own claims.

THE PRC'S PERSPECTIVE ON REUNIFICATION

Peaceful unification, or reunification as the PRC describes it, was put on the agenda on New Year's Day in 1979. The Standing Committee of the National People's Congress addressed an open letter to "Taiwan compatriots" that shared the hope that "Taiwan will soon rejoin the motherland in accomplishing the great task of nation building". Among other things it proposed visits by separated families and opening up trade as mechanisms to begin the process of reconciliation. Until this point, the PRC had only spoken about "liberating Taiwan", implying subsuming Taiwan by force of military intervention. It was an extraordinary communication at a pivotal moment. Mao was dead, Deng Xiaoping had introduced the transformative idea of "reform and opening" and the PRC was riding a wave of diplomatic successes, including the establishment of relations with the US and Japan. After decades of self-imposed isolation and domestic suffering, the PRC was re-entering the world and contemplating the long-delayed task of national unification.

The letter itself was full of emotion, referencing the pain of separation and empathy for homesick exiled "compatriots" longing for the motherland. The tone evinced confidence in the historical inevitability of unification and lent heavily on the civilizational, cultural and ethnic responsibility of "compatriots" in Taiwan to the Chinese nation. It invoked the mythological common origins of the Chinese nation as "descendants of the Yellow Emperor" and equated rejection of unification with betrayal of "our ancestors". The letter announced the cessation of PLA shelling of Taiwan-held Kinmen island off the Chinese coast and made it possible to talk of "cross-Strait relations". Notably it called on the authorities in Taiwan to accede to the shared wishes of the people of the PRC and Taiwan to rejoin the single family under the Chinese nation.

The letter was soon followed by a policy of "three links" and "four exchanges", reversing the previous decades' frozen connections. The KMT government in Taiwan did not reciprocate, however, and formally resisted establishing such links until the 2000s. In September 1981, the chair of the NPC Standing Committee Ye Jianying, announced "Nine Principles for Peaceful Reunification". It was the first attempt to sketch out a proposal of the form unification might take. It envisaged a high degree of autonomy for Taiwan, with guarantees for Taiwan's economic and social organization and individual rights.

A few months later, Deng Xiaoping summarized Ye's Nine Principles as embodying a new form of national administration that could be characterized as "one country, two systems": the first mention of the system that was originally formulated with Taiwan in mind, but would become famous for providing a solution to the retrocession of Hong Kong to the PRC in 1997. By the end of 1982, an amended PRC constitution provided for the establishment of special administrative regions with administrative systems suited to practical conditions. In effect, this was the legal foundation for "one country, two systems". However, the KMT government continued to reject PRC overtures and for the next decade retained a hostile attitude of "no contact, no negotiation and no compromise".

Unification on the PRC's terms, notwithstanding their ostensible flexibility, would mean relinquishing ROC sovereignty, something that was inconceivable and intolerable for the KMT regime. President Chiang Ching-kuo did however admit the possibility of future unification on the basis of Sun Yat-sen's Three Principles of the People (a condition that was not likely to be met any time soon) and dropped the ROC's warlike rhetoric of "counterattack" and "recovering the mainland".

The new openness in the PRC was welcoming to people in Taiwan with family ties, business ideas and capital to invest. Although technically forbidden by the ROC government, social and economic interactions between the two sides – albeit flowing in one direction, from Taiwan to the PRC – flourished. In 1987, a landmark year in Taiwan with the rescinding of martial law, restrictions were lifted on private visits to the PRC. The ROC was extremely cautious in loosening its regulation of contact with the PRC, but this one act opened what would eventually become a flood gate of economic and social exchange.

Chiang Ching-kuo's death in 1989, and the subsequent rise of Lee Teng-hui to ROC president, ushered in another new phase in cross-Strait relations (Roy 2003). It is curious looking back at Lee Teng-hui's early years as then-unelected ROC president and comparing his words and deeds to the pro-Taiwan independence figure he would resemble a decade later. In his inaugural address in 1990 entitled "Opening a New Era for the Chinese People", Lee affirmed that "Taiwan and the mainland are indivisible parts of Chinese territory" and called on people on both sides to work together toward "our common goal of national unification". The wrinkle in Lee's position, which would be the ROC's over the ensuing decade, was that Taiwan would comprehensively open up economic and social exchange if the PRC demonstrated progress toward political democratization, economic liberalization and renounced the use of force against Taiwan. If these were enacted, when the conditions were right, Taiwan would be willing to enter talks about unification on the basis of equality.

Given that Lee's message was delivered soon after the Democracy Movement was brutally suppressed in Tiananmen Square, the ROC's condition that unification talks were predicated on democratization in the PRC was unforeseeable. However, Lee established the National Unification Council, an advisory body representing various interests, which issued the Guidelines for National Unification in 1991. The Guidelines included short- to long-term measures for trust building and exchanges leading ultimately to unification talks. They included explicit adherence to One China and led to the establishment of the semi-official Straits Exchange Foundation (SEF), a non-governmental body authorized to conduct dialogue and represent the ROC government in administrative dealings with the equivalent PRC organization, the Association for Relations Across the Taiwan Straits (ARATS).

These organizations removed the need for the two governments to meet directly, and became the vehicle for extensive liberalization of cross-Strait interactions during the 1990s. When the ROC ended its Temporary Provisions in 1991 and adopted a new law to govern relations between people on both sides of the Strait in 1992, it signalled a new openness to economic and social exchange. Despite the PRC's refusal to renounce the use of force based on fears about external influence and "independence forces", there was sufficient common ground and momentum for representatives of Taiwan's SEF and the PRC's ARATS to meet in Singapore in 1993. This was the first official meeting between the two sides. It was facilitated by secret contacts in Hong Kong in 1992 and overcame fraught negotiations, mistrust and fears of misinterpreted signals. When SEF chair Koo Chen-fu and ARATS chair Wang Daohan met in Singapore, "political issues" were explicitly and deliberately left off the agenda. However, the two sides agreed on a number of practical arrangements that would help regulate already existing informal cross-Strait exchanges and open others.

Given the lack of contact and state of enmity and distrust that existed, the Koo–Wang talks were a significant milestone. But the lack of common ground was soon concretized by the publication of the PRC's 1993 white paper on "The Taiwan Question and the Reunification of China", which confirmed that "one country, two systems" was the PRC's only offer. It also reaffirmed the PRC's primacy in the concept of reunification, i.e. the ROC would be subsumed into the PRC and any pretension to ROC sovereignty would have to be relinquished. These developments symbolized the progress in cross-Strait relations over the next decades: incremental opening up and intensification of economic and social interactions combined with irreconcilable political positions.

As businesses on both sides energetically exploited economic complementarities, governments gradually made adjustments to react to realities on the ground. This generally involved unilateral moves to legalize or regulate trade, travel and other practical issues that were already happening. During the 1990s and early 2000s the economic momentum was so powerful that not even ongoing political stalemate could hinder progress toward economic interdependence. Even as Lee Teng-hui's visit to Cornell University prompted the missile crisis of 1995–96, trade and investment grew to monumental proportions. Chen Shui-bian was castigated by the PRC for his purported advocacy of "Taiwan independence", but it was under Chen that progress was made toward establishing the "Three Links" (postal, commercial and transportation) first proposed by the PRC in 1979 and resisted by the ROC until 2001. After Chen gave the go ahead for the mini-Three Links, Ma Ying-jeou finally okayed the full version in 2008. The result of these progressive openings was that the PRC became Taiwan's biggest trade partner, registering more than double the amount of trade of the second-placed US. For a time, more than a million Taiwanese professionals and businesspeople (known as *Taishang*) resided more or less permanently in China.

The extent of these cross-Strait connections had always been a source of concern in Taiwan. Not least because the PRC was explicit about linking economics and politics. The idea was that economic integration would spill over into closer political ties. Failing that, the scale of Taiwanese businesses' investments and exposure to the Chinese market would produce useful leverage that the PRC could use to influence Taiwanese politics. Neither happened, as we shall discuss in a later chapter. Indeed, as the two economies became more entwined, culminating in the ECFA free trade agreement signed during Ma's first term, popular support for unification in Taiwan plummeted.

Despite fears of "hollowed out" manufacturing, industrial espionage, intellectual property theft, and Chinese investments that would distort Taipei's real estate market, Taiwan has effectively inoculated itself from economic interdependence becoming a political vulnerability. In part, by resisting fully liberalized cross-Strait trade and investment. Taiwanese businesspeople did not become the "fifth column" some feared they would (Keng & Schubert 2010). Rising costs, difficult operating conditions and homegrown PRC competitors prompted many Taiwanese companies to relocate or return home. Taiwan managed to keep its crown jewel semiconductor firms at home.

Ultimately the PRC has pushed for various types of unification through economic and political means. Some of these attempts were more successful in linking the two sides of the Strait, while others led to backlash and damaged cross-Strait relations. Given the changes in Taiwanese identity, nationalistic or cultural calls for unification increasingly fall on deaf ears. The worry observers have now is under what conditions the PRC may feel the need to use military means to bring about unification.

TAIWAN IN CHINESE NATIONALISM

During China's reform era since 1978, Taiwan has become a central focus of Chinese nationalism (Hughes 1997). More broadly conceived, Chinese nationalism itself has become one of the major pillars of CCP legitimacy. The CCP narrative about Taiwan, that it has been an inalienable part of Chinese territory since ancient times and its current separation is due to colonial aggression, foreign interference and treasonous separatists like Lee Teng-hui and Tsai Ing-wen, is consistent with a broader narrative about "national humiliation" (when China was weak) and "national rejuvenation" (now that China is strong again under the CCP's rule).

The continuation of the CCP regime requires a compelling narrative to retain popular support. Decades of economic growth and modernization, and tangible improvements in material well-being for most Chinese people, have generated a store of performance legitimacy. But economic performance alone was insufficient to secure popular acquiescence to continuing authoritarian circumscriptions and the impossibility of political liberalization. In the decades after the violent denouement of the student movement and workers' protests in and around Tiananmen Square in the summer of 1989, the regime sought to systematically inculcate patriotism and to connect love of the Chinese nation to the fortunes of the CCP-led party-state (Wang 2008).

Through constant reinforcement, and the suppression of alternative narratives, the regime has tied the fortunes of the nation to the party. The regime has successfully established in the popular imagination that hostile forces are determined to hinder the "sacred task" of national unification. Conceived as a battle waged on China by hostile Others, many elements in foreign affairs can be viewed through this lens, but Taiwan, with its additional constructions of familial separation, common ancestry and disrupted destiny is the most powerful.

Official discourse in the PRC reflects transposed elements of Marxist theory, where history is driven by continuous open-ended struggle and an inherent logic of development. Localized through "socialism with Chinese characteristics", discourse around the PRC's modernization has adopted not just Marxist ideas about history and progress, but those infused with nationalism and more traditional Chinese culture. The end result, when it comes to Taiwan, is a utopian vision of national unification as the culmination of "the Chinese Dream" and "great rejuvenation of the Chinese nation". Yet, unlike other grand national projects with utopian elements, like the Belt and Road Initiative, "the Taiwan question" is bounded by an endpoint, namely unification.

Given the definitive quality of unification – Taiwan is either under PRC control or not – the CCP has set a tangible marker for its own performance legitimacy. Making unification the bottom line for the claims it makes about being the true champion and defender of the Chinese nation reduces the CCP's room for manoeuvre. Having explicitly established the stakes, and convinced the Chinese people it will do everything in its power to prevail, the party cannot afford to soften its hardline positions on Taiwan.

In official discourse about Taiwan, the party expresses confidence in the realization of unification as a national quest. Officials employ temporal markers and time horizons to cultivate a sense of inevitability of unification, offering succour to domestic audiences who have been promised this outcome. Such constructions are also designed to undermine the resolve of Taiwanese people and convince them that resistance to the historical process of unification is futile.

Notwithstanding repeated statements that "the historic goal of reuniting our motherland must be realised and will be realised", progress toward "peaceful unification" has floundered. Taiwanese public opinion has gone monotonically away from unification over the last three decades (see Chapter X). Contrary to PRC expectations that Taiwanese people would find the prospect of unification enhanced by the stunning success of Chinese development and economic transformation, they have instead expressed a decreasing appetite for renouncing ROC sovereignty or risking hard-won rights and values guaranteed by Taiwan's democratic system. In an ever larger number Taiwanese people express their identity preferences in a way that undermines the likelihood they will voluntarily choose unification.

Instead of questioning why Taiwanese people ascribe such value to Taiwan's de facto independence, even in the face of threats from the PRC, the CCP has chosen to foreground the purported role of "separatist forces" and "external interference". It is easier to deflect blame onto such exogenous factors than to question why the PRC regime has failed to win Taiwanese hearts and minds, despite what it considers the generous offer of a "one country, two systems" solution. In conversations with PRC officials, they have expressed perplexity that Taiwanese are unwilling to accept a pragmatic solution that would immediately give Taiwan access to the things Taiwanese people say they desire: security, international participation, national respect. These officials' puzzlement is symptomatic of a basic inability to empathize with Taiwanese people and to understand how they perceive themselves and what they ascribe value to. It also reflects limited self-awareness about the effects of the PRC's own actions, within China and toward Taiwan. How actions in Hong Kong, say, reduce Taiwan's faith and confidence in the PRC's pledge to protect the "rights and interests of the people in Taiwan" in the event of unification.

In popular expressions about Taiwan that flood Chinese digital spaces, the tone that veers between jeering and beseeching, anger and quasi-familial yearning, is fuelled by the dissonance generated by the reality of Taiwan's ongoing separation and hegemonic official narratives about unstoppable progress and the inevitability of unification. The disconnect between hardline popular nationalist positions on Taiwan – such as the wave of extreme voices that accompanied US Speaker Pelosi's visit in August 2022 – and official support for "peaceful unification" is difficult for the regime to balance. This balancing act helps explain the large-scale PLA live-fire drills that followed Pelosi's visit. And it is reflected in the contradiction of accelerated capacity-building for future coercive contingencies while promising a respectful and fair transition to "one country, two systems".

The CCP regime has become frustrated, impatient and concerned that Taiwan's separation could be prolonged into an unpredictable future. This danger is compounded by the increasing international salience of Taiwan, and the support that Taiwan's "existing independence" refining of the "status quo" has generated in many western capitals. Having invested so much political capital in unification this represents a substantial risk to the regime's legitimacy claims.

It also reveals how the PRC under Xi Jinping perceives its position in the world. Under Xi, PRC foreign policy has pivoted to a "new model of major country diplomacy", jettisoning Deng and his immediate successors' more cautious posture. "Hide and bide" has been replaced by "the confident rise". Deng's notion of "ascending the heights and taking a long-term perspective" with regard to Taiwan, i.e. putting off resolution of the issue to future generations, has also fallen out of favour. Confident in China's new-found economic and military strength, Xi has explicitly rejected Deng's patience. In his January 2019 speech marking the 40th anniversary of the "message to Taiwan compatriots", Xi revealed his impatience, saying that "the political division across the Strait cannot be passed on from generation to generation".

While Xi has not set a timetable for unification, 2049 is the deadline for "national rejuvenation", a project from which unification is an indivisible part. Given the stakes, and the failure of the PRC's proposal for unification to gain any traction in Taiwan at the elite or mass level, it is not surprising that the PRC's policy towards Taiwan has hardened. Economic interdependence did not spill over into politics; familiarity borne of intensive people-to-people exchanges did not increase the PRC's attractiveness; preferential visas and investment rules did not lead to a cohort of unification-supporting young people. The consequence of these outcomes is a recalibration of the policy of carrots and sticks, with an intensification of pressures on Taiwan across all sectors.

6

One China, multiple considerations

What is the US position with regard to Taiwan? Due to Taiwan's contested and unrecognized status, and the ambiguities that the US has deliberately cultivated, the answer is not straightforward. The Taiwan issue abounds in complications, such as the subtle difference between the US' "One-China policy" and the PRC's "One-China principle". In this chapter we set out the "Taiwan Relations Act", the "Three Joint Communiques" and "Six Assurances" that have formed the US framework for handling Taiwan and China relations since the 1970s. We also discuss the US' posture of "strategic ambiguity", a useful position that has recently come under pressure from within the US. Demystifying these concepts and terminology is fundamental to understanding the US position. In this chapter, we explain the history of the US–Taiwan relationship, how key US–Taiwan policy was formed, and how these policies are used in practice today.

FROM ROC TO PRC: HOW THE UNITED STATES CAME TO NOT RECOGNIZE TAIWAN

During the Chinese Civil War (technically 1945–49, but fought intermittently since the 1920s), the US and most of the western world supported and backed the KMT side against the CCP. Even after the Civil War ended and the KMT fled to Taiwan, the US continued to support the KMT's claim to represent the legitimate government of China. Despite being exiled to Taiwan and possessing no authority over Chinese territory, the ROC on Taiwan was still seen as the "true" China by much of the world. At the United Nations and other international organizations the ROC was recognized as the governing body of China for several decades. The advent of the Korean War in the summer of 1950 sealed the US' determination to support the ROC and prevent the PLA from invading and taking control of Taiwan. The US provided training for Chiang's Nationalist Army, substantial military aid and technical assistance, and ultimately signed a mutual defence treaty with the ROC in 1954.

In the same period, the PRC underwent dramatic changes. After its founding in 1949, the PRC experienced new levels of state and nation building, but also devastating events like the Great Leap Forward (1958–60) and the Cultural Revolution (1966–76). Much as he wanted to in the years after 1949, Mao never gained authority over Taiwan. However, developments in US–PRC relations towards the latter part of Mao's reign had the effect of baking Taiwan into contemporary PRC nationalism. In the 1970s, the United States began carefully angling for rapprochement with the PRC, seeking to make strategic gains from China's split with the USSR. The formal normalization of relations between the US and the PRC took years of negotiation, but would fundamentally alter the US–China–Taiwan triangle.

The US formally recognized the PRC in 1979. The US simultaneously de-recognized the ROC, which would progressively lose international recognition as the legitimate governing body of China. The ROC would no longer have access to representation at the United Nations, and other countries were forced to choose which "China" they wanted to have diplomatic relations with. As the PRC became stronger and richer, the number of countries choosing to recognize the ROC instead of the PRC declined, to the handful still doing so today.

However, the need to choose Beijing or Taipei in terms of establishing formal ties did not mean the end of other kinds of relations with the ROC. In the case of the US, it began a new phase of *unofficial* relations. Even though the US changed which side it recognized as the official China, it continued to enjoy (intensive) economic, social and informal diplomatic interactions with the ROC. Irrespective of diplomatic formalities, the US retained a strategic interest in Taiwan remaining outside the direct control of and unaligned with the PRC. That enduring strategic interest took on an extra dimension as Taiwan underwent democratization and became an established democracy.

Because relations are unofficial, the language, grammar and syntax often seem convoluted, deliberately passive and confusing. For example, US policy does not refer to the Taiwanese government or the Taiwanese people directly. Instead, it uses constructions like "the governing authorities on Taiwan" or "the people on Taiwan". Even for longstanding experts on the Asia-Pacific it can be difficult to nail down what policies are or the correct way to frame them. Our goal here is to add some clarity.

THE THREE COMMUNIQUÉS, TAIWAN RELATIONS ACT (TRA) AND THE SIX ASSURANCES

These three documents are the fundamental components that have shaped and defined the US–Taiwan relationship over the past four decades. Often formal readouts from the White House begin or conclude with the line "in accordance with the TRA, Three Communiqués and Six Assurances". Understanding what each one means, and what they do not, is an important first step to demystifying US–Taiwan relations. In recent years, the US has tended to give extra emphasis to the TRA, a political choice, but we deal with them here in chronological order.

The Three Communiqués

The Three Communiqués, joint statements by the governments of the US and PRC, were issued in 1972, 1979 and 1982 respectively. These three joint statements help delineate the expectations that the US and PRC held for US–Taiwan policy. Chronologically, the TRA comes between Communiqués 2 and 3, which is the order in which we deal with them here since it gives a sense of how the US position evolved.

Communiqué 1: the Shanghai Communiqué, 27 February 1972

The First Communiqué, also called the Shanghai Communiqué, resulted from a meeting between President Richard Nixon and PRC Premier Zhou Enlai, following Nixon's ground-breaking visit to China and meeting with Chairman Mao. Its content goes beyond US–Taiwan relations, since the meeting was conducted at a time when the US was trying to normalize relations with the PRC. But Taiwan was a major factor preventing normalization, which led to this attempt to smooth a way forward. The most relevant passage for US–Taiwan relations can be summarized as follows: the United States *acknowledges* that all Chinese on either side of the Taiwan Strait maintain there is but one China and that Taiwan is a part of China, and the US does not challenge that position.[1] China meanwhile firmly opposes any separation of Taiwan either as an independent country or as a second China, and that the question of Taiwan is an internal matter for China to decide, not the US.[2]

The statement may seem contradictory, or that the two sides are talking past each other, but it remains a fundamental starting point to how the US began its approach to dealing with China's claims over Taiwan. The US *acknowledges* the PRC's claims, but does not *accept* or *endorse* those claims. This is not pedantic word play, since in the world of foreign policy and diplomacy the difference between *acknowledge* and *recognize* is critical. By acknowledging China's claims, the US demonstrated respect for the PRC's preference. But by not accepting it, the US retains the potential to support alternatives, including defending Taiwan from the PRC's claims.

Communiqué 2: normalization of US–PRC relations, 1 January 1979

In a televised New Year's Day address to the American public and a global audience, President Jimmy Carter announced that the US was to establish formal diplomatic ties with the PRC for the first time. The US

---

1. This nuance of "All Chinese on either side of the Strait" confuses people in both Taiwan and the US, since fewer and fewer people in Taiwan see themselves as Chinese. How US policy ought to adapt given the nature of Taiwan's changing national identity is a continuous yet key problem for policymakers who want policies that match the reality of Taiwan on the ground.
2. The full text for this communiqué and other Taiwan–US policy documents are available online at the American Institute in Taiwan's website, https://www.ait.org.tw/.

and PRC released a joint statement that formally established that the US would recognize the PRC instead of the ROC. Within the declaration, the US reiterated acknowledgement of the PRC's claims, but did not formally recognize them.[3] Such inconsistencies and obfuscations in language would later create discord and confusion in articulating where the US and PRC stand on each other's claims (Garver 2015).

It cannot be overstated how ground-breaking the US's rapprochement with the PRC was for international politics. By normalizing relations with the PRC, the United States cemented a trend of bringing the PRC out of international isolation and into the global order. It also signalled the terminal decline of the ROC's formal international presence. By establishing relations with the PRC, the United States had to immediately withdraw military personnel from Taiwan and end all former military defence treaties signed with the ROC. Taiwanese and Americans in Taiwan had no forewarning of the establishment of formal relations with the PRC, and learned of the diplomatic shift at the same time as television viewers in the US. The news shocked the KMT regime and Taiwanese people, who naturally feared what it would mean for the ROC's security and survival.

The Taiwan Relations Act, 10 April 1979 (retroactively effective 1 January 1979)

Several months after normalization and the end of formal diplomatic relations with the ROC, the US Congress passed the Taiwan Relations Act (TRA) into law. A diverse coalition of members of Congress mobilized in reaction to a staunch anti-communist ally suddenly made vulnerable by the normalization agreement. A further stimulus was the lack of White House consultation with Congress, against the backdrop of the Vietnam War, which prompted a unique legislative response in the realm of US security and foreign relations. The TRA was the result of bipartisan cooperation in Congress which quickly drafted and almost

---

3. In the PRC's official readout of the communiqué, the Mandarin for "acknowledge" was used instead of "recognize", diverging from the Chinese used to describe the same English in the 1972 Communiqué (Drun 2017).

unanimously passed it into law. The TRA outlined and defined how the US would conduct newly unofficial relations with Taiwan. The key policy points are as follows:

1. Promote economic, cultural and political ties between the United States, Taiwan and China.
2. Peace and security in the Taiwan Strait are an important interest of the United States.
3. Formal relations with the PRC are contingent on the future of Taiwan's status being resolved peacefully.
4. Any non-peaceful attempts to resolve Taiwan's status will be of serious concern to the US.
5. The United States will sell arms "of a defensive character" to Taiwan.
6. The United States will push back against any forces that try to jeopardize the social and economic well-being of the Taiwanese people.

Other parts of the TRA outline basic institutions of the US–Taiwan relationship like the American Institute in Taiwan, the US's de facto embassy in Taiwan, and how the president and Congress are to conduct themselves when carrying out or changing the TRA's policies.

The TRA does not mention whether or not the US takes a position on "unification" or "independence". Instead, it emphasizes that resolution of Taiwan's contested status should be achieved by peaceful means. It also emphasizes the "defensive" nature of arms sales to Taiwan. The stated purpose of selling weapons to Taiwan was explicitly not to increase Taiwan's capacity to attack China (or any other state). Instead, it was focused solely on ensuring that Taiwan would be able to defend itself in the event of an attack. In doing so, the US created a space in which its commitment to defend Taiwan under various contingencies could remain strategically ambiguous.

Communiqué 3, 17 August 1982

The final Communiqué, issued in 1982, addressed US arms sales to Taiwan. The PRC was adamantly opposed to this practice, irrespective of American claims that the weapons were designed for defensive purposes. The US attempted to assuage PRC concerns by stating that it hoped not to sell arms to Taiwan in the long term, and that the type and quantity of weapons sold to Taiwan would not change after the normalization of relations between the US and PRC. Implicit in the US position, but not explicitly agreed to by the PRC, was that the reduction of arms sales would be contingent on the PRC's actions and a commitment to a peaceful resolution of the Taiwan question. In other words, the US position was that it would only reduce arms sales if the PRC demonstrated a commitment to peace. Notwithstanding the PRC's preference for "peaceful unification", the PRC never renounced the right to use force. Since this equation was ambiguous, it left the interpretation of what constituted a commitment to peace open, and by extension, room for the US to modify the level of support it provided to Taiwan (Ross 1997). This ambiguity has been leveraged in recent years as the US' evaluation of the PRC commitment to peace has been revised, and its willingness to sell weapons to Taiwan has increased accordingly. When this joint statement was released, both the US and the PRC re-emphasized the contents of the previous two communiqués as well.

The Six Assurances, 17 August 1982

A striking feature of the Three Communiqués is the absence of any Taiwanese voice or agency in any of the agreements. Indeed, during this time the ROC had little say in how the PRC or the US were crafting their joint statements. This naturally made the Taiwanese government uneasy. The Third Communiqué in particular made the KMT authoritarian government worried, as it hinted at the possible end of the US' willingness to help defend Taiwan. In 1982, the KMT entered into negotiations with its American counterparts. The result was Six Assurances that would help guide US policy towards Taiwan. The United States

1. would not set a date to end arms sales to Taiwan;
2. will not consult the PRC over arms sales to Taiwan;
3. will not try to mediate Taiwan–China relations;
4. would not revise the TRA;

5. would not change its position on the PRC's sovereignty over Taiwan;
6. would not pressure Taiwan into entering negotiations with the PRC.

There is some debate about the specific wording of the assurances. When they were announced the wording varied slightly between how the US conveyed the contents to Taiwan, how it was conveyed by the White House to Congress, and how the KMT framed the assurances to the Taiwanese public (Lawrence 2020).

THE US' ONE-CHINA POLICY VS THE PRC'S ONE-CHINA PRINCIPLE

The foundations of the American One-China policy are that the US *acknowledges* the PRC's claims over Taiwan, but does not *accept* the PRC claim to Taiwan, that the US will continue to maintain strong but *unofficial* relations with the ROC, while also advocating for a peaceful resolution to the fundamental disagreement on either side of the Taiwan Strait. The official position on Taiwan's status is that it is unresolved, and that the US does not take a position on the issue of sovereignty (Bush 2017).

The One-China policy is not the same as the One-China principle (Chen 2022). The latter embodies the PRC's stance over the question of Taiwan. Its clearest articulation came in 2000 from the PRC's Taiwan Affairs Office, which stated that since 1949 the PRC has held a One-China principle that there is only one China and that Taiwan is part of that China, that Taiwan is an integral part of Chinese territory, and the PRC will not tolerate or accept any future in which Taiwan is seen as separate from China. Furthermore, it is the PRC's goal to "peacefully reunify" with Taiwan using a "one country, two systems" framework similar to that of Hong Kong.

The US' One-China policy and the PRC's One-China principle are often conflated or confused. Reporters, authors and even politicians sometimes incorrectly imply that the US or PRC adhere to the other's Policy/Principle, or claim that the US accepts that Taiwan is part of

China. PRC officials and news outlets are wont to imply that the US abides by the One-China principle, when it in fact does not. Many other countries have their own specific version of a "One-China policy" or a "One-China principle" that generally falls somewhere on a spectrum between those of the US and the PRC. For example, Japan's One-China policy says it "respects" China's claims but does not say it accepts their claims.

Part of the reason for the confusion between how China and the US see the One-China principle and One-China policy is translation. When the US announces its One-China policy and adheres to the stance that it *acknowledges* but does not *accept* China's claims over Taiwan, the PRC will often use language in Mandarin that implies that the US is more supportive of the PRC's claims than it actually is. The US' One-China policy is not the only one to suffer a loss of precision in translation, which is why there is often disagreement followed by retroactive statements on One China between different countries and the PRC. Often it is a matter of countries specifying that they do not actually adhere to the PRC's One-China principle.

STRATEGIC AMBIGUITY

There is no formal version of the US' One-China policy contained in a single written document. Instead, it is considered to be the amalgamation of the TRA, the Three Communiqués, and the Six Assurances. If the lack of a formally written One-China policy makes the US stance on Taiwan seem ambiguous, that is because it is purposefully so. Ambiguity is perhaps one of the biggest and most important strategies the US has employed in articulating its relationship with Taiwan (Tucker 2005). Although the phrase is frequently invoked, there is often misunderstanding about what strategic ambiguity is and is not. Like the One-China policy, there is no formal policy document that states explicitly what strategic ambiguity is. However, over time it has been interpreted by policymakers and analysts relatively consistently.

Strategic ambiguity boils down to whether or not the US would come to Taiwan's aid in the event of a military conflict between the PRC and ROC. The "ambiguity" is about remaining deliberately unclear on whether or not the US military would join a conflict. Under certain conditions, it is implied that the US would be more likely to defend Taiwan. For example, if the PRC attacked unprovoked then the US would be more likely to come to Taiwan's aid. If Taiwan was to directly provoke the PRC by making a unilateral declaration of independence, then the US would perhaps be less likely to come to Taiwan's defence.

What is the aim of this strategy? Why would the US devise a policy that tries to both accommodate and deter the PRC and ROC? From the perspective of the US–China relationship it gives the PRC assurances that the US is not inevitably tying its military presence to Taiwan. Instead, the US would only employ its military in the event of an unprovoked attack. From the US–Taiwan perspective, it reminds Taiwan that it does not have carte blanche with regard to US military support. In other words, Taiwan cannot assume that the US will send its military to defend Taiwan, thereby giving Taiwan the freedom to act and do as it pleases knowing the US has its back no matter what.

To a degree, strategic ambiguity was as much about deterrence as it is about the US keeping its options open. The goal is to deter the PRC from committing to military conflict over Taiwan, because the United States may intervene. It is also about deterring Taiwan from unilaterally declaring independence. The US goal is to have relations of varying degrees across different sectors with both the PRC and ROC. Employing ambiguous policies allows the US to do so in a way that does not egregiously offend or empower either side.

Strategic ambiguity is *not* about whether the US supports or wants relations with Taiwan. The US is not at all ambiguous in its support for Taiwan's democracy or Taiwan's right to exist. Neither is the US ambiguous about its intentions to foster *unofficial* but *meaningful* relations with Taiwan. Even though much of the US' One-China policy towards Taiwan is ambiguous, strategic ambiguity is not about the One-China policy, only about American military commitment (Tucker & Glaser 2011).

CHALLENGES TO STRATEGIC AMBIGUITY

One of the issues with unwritten policies is that they rely on verbal conventions that are sometimes contradicted. One prominent example is the contradiction between insistence that the US military would not inevitably defend Taiwan in conflict and variation in the formulations used by various presidents to depict the US' commitments to Taiwan. Despite the best efforts of White House officials and Taiwan policy analysts to maintain consistency in the policy of strategic ambiguity, numerous American presidents have inadvertently called the policy into question.

The first time strategic ambiguity was called into question was during George W. Bush's tenure as president in 2001. During a televised interview, President Bush pledged that the US would "do whatever it takes" to defend Taiwan. This was immediately interpreted as a departure from strategic ambiguity, and it was inferred that the US would defend Taiwan no matter what. Soon after, the White House put out a statement that the US One-China policy had not in fact changed.

In 2016, president-elect Donald Trump accepted a congratulatory phone call from ROC president Tsai Ing-wen. This broke a number of precedents for US–Taiwan relations. For one, the US president does not directly communicate with the Taiwanese president as part of unofficial relations, a self-imposed policy that had been maintained since the Second Communiqué in 1979. More importantly, however, was that following the call president-elect Trump called the One-China policy into question. He tweeted "I don't know why we have to be bound by a 'one China' policy unless we make a deal with China having to do with other things, including trade". For a moment, this put the world of Taiwan policymakers on alert, since this kind of statement jeopardizes the uneasy peace that US policymakers had spent decades trying to establish and maintain. Moreover, the US position on Taiwan was never meant, as Trump seemed to be implying, to be an economic bargaining chip with China. Soon after Trump's tweet, White House officials put out a statement declaring that the US still abided by the One-China policy and that there had been no policy change. Later, President Trump said that he had "agreed, at the request of President Xi, to honour our 'one China' policy". However, loose and sometimes inflammatory language recurred throughout Trump's term in office. Leading figures in the former Trump administration have continued to voice incautious and unhelpful sentiments, such as former secretary of state Mike Pompeo's call for the US to formally recognize Taiwan.

Further confusion over the US policy of strategic ambiguity was created by President Joe Biden. After taking office in January 2021, President Biden called strategic ambiguity into question on multiple occasions. In August 2021, he said in an interview that the US would respond to military action against Taiwan in the same way as it would with South Korea, Japan or any NATO ally. The implication was that Taiwan held the same status in US foreign policy as one of these official relationships (ABC News 2021). In October 2021, when asked "can you vow to protect Taiwan?" President Biden responded "Yes". When asked for clarification, "You are saying that the United States would come to Taiwan's defence if China attacked?", Biden said "Yes, we have committed to do that". The long-term US policy toward Taiwan does not include such a commitment (White House 2021). In May 2022, when asked "Are you willing to get involved militarily to defend Taiwan if it comes to that?", President Biden again responded, "Yes, that's the commitment we made" (Ward & Forgey 2022). And in September 2022, Biden said during an interview that "The US military would defend Taiwan if there was an unprecedented attack against Taiwan" (Ward & Forgey 2022). After each of Biden's comments, the White House immediately put out statements to the effect that the US had not changed its policy towards Taiwan, and that the president's comments do not indicate a change in policy.

There are two ways to understand Biden's comments. If we understand strategic ambiguity as a policy indicating that under certain conditions the US would defend Taiwan against an attack from China, then some of Biden's comments do not inherently contradict US policy. For example, in his September 2022 remark, the US supporting Taiwan during an "unprecedented attack" could be read as consistent with strategic ambiguity, which implies that the US would likely defend Taiwan if China attacked unprovoked. Yet, Biden's comments implying Taiwan's equivalence to NATO allies contradict US policy. For some analysts, including in the PRC, these comments were taken as a challenge to strategic ambiguity and a sign that the US is moving away from strategic ambiguity and towards a new policy of "strategic clarity".

Strategic clarity would involve the US stating explicitly and categorically that it would defend Taiwan from a military attack by China. For some American politicians and analysts, this change in policy is necessitated by the PRC's increasing aggression towards Taiwan over the past few years. It is also more consistent with how Biden has portrayed US policy towards Taiwan. Proponents of strategic ambiguity argue that removing the policy would increase the potential for conflict in the Taiwan Strait. The debate between the need to adhere to ambiguity versus switching to clarity has been a feature of discussion among Taiwan analysts and policymakers for years (Glaser *et al.* 2020). Switching to strategic clarity would signal to the PRC that the US is committed to involvement in a military conflict in the Taiwan Strait were China to initiate it. For some, this move could be seen as a deterrent to conflict because it commits the US military. For others, it is seen as an incentive for the PRC to attack, because a firm US military commitment could be considered a "red line" by China.

TAIWAN IN AMERICAN PARTY POLITICS

One longstanding misconception about Taiwan policy in the US is that the Republican Party is strong on Taiwan and the Democratic Party is weak. Voting records in the House of Representatives and Senate show that consistently, across administrations and policy sectors, both Republicans and Democrats voting across party lines in favour of Taiwan policy. The idea that one party is more supportive than the other does not survive scrutiny of the voting record. Nor is there much difference in the parties' provision of forms of symbolic support to Taiwan. Delegations from the US to Taiwan are consistently bipartisan, led by different parties and made up of politicians with different political values who come together over American support for Taiwan. Perhaps no two better examples demonstrate this level of bipartisan support than that of Mike Pompeo and Nancy Pelosi. Despite their seemingly incompatible stances on US domestic politics, both have shown through their delegation visits a commitment to Taiwan.

The misconception that Republicans are more supportive of Taiwan likely derives from the louder volume at which they advocate for Taiwan, especially since the Trump administration. Indeed, there was a significant intensification of Taiwan policy during the Trump administration, during which arms sales to Taiwan almost doubled compared to the Obama and Bush administrations. In light of the growing US–China rivalry, Republicans also became more willing to openly criticize China and promote Taiwan rhetorically. But Republican vociferousness on Taiwan should not be equated with Democrat tepidness or weakness toward Taiwan. After Joe Biden entered office he continued Trump's more robust policies towards Taiwan. Voting on bills related to Taiwan has also remained consistent regardless of whether the presidency is held by Republican or Democrat. Amid high levels of polarization in American politics, Taiwan is one of the few issues to enjoy bipartisan consensus.

TAIWAN AND AMERICAN "CONTAINMENT" OF CHINA

The PRC's frustration that progress toward national unification has not proceeded as it hoped is directed particularly at "external interference" by "anti-China forces" (meaning the US) and "separatist forces" within Taiwan (particularly the DPP). From the PRC perspective, American support for Taiwan is the fundamental source of nourishment that allowed the possibility of "Taiwan independence" to grow. The dual deterrence inherent in the guiding philosophy of American strategic ambiguity has successfully limited coercive moves by the PRC *and* the possibility of a Taiwanese declaration of independence for four decades (Ross 2002). Yet seen from the PRC side, it is America's willingness to supply "weapons of a defensive nature" to Taiwan as part of the TRA that has stymied progress towards unification. Without this assistance, Taiwan would not have been in a position to resist or to consider pro-longed separation a feasible option. The PRC frames this as part of a broader American refusal to accept "China's rise", and a strategy to limit or "contain" Chinese development.

The PRC can point to examples of what it considers American inter-ference in this "internal affair of China" going back decades. In 1950, with the advent of the Korean War and after PRC forces had already retaken Hainan Island and were threatening an attack on Taiwan, President Truman dispatched the Seventh Fleet to the Taiwan Strait to prevent an invasion. A mutual defence treaty followed in 1954.[4] The

---

4. Text available at https://avalon.law.yale.edu/20th_century/chin001.asp.

ambiguous status quo of a diplomatically unrecognized PRC in control of China and an émigré ROC restricted to Taiwan was effectively locked in by the security guarantees given to the ROC by the US following the Korean War. Thereafter the PRC and ROC waged a miniature cold war of their own.

American strategic ambiguity was beneficial to the PRC, because it allowed the country to focus on the "opening and reform" policies that would spark its economic transformation rather than mobilizing for war to prevent "Taiwan independence". The PRC also benefited enormously from American economic engagement policies. Even after a brief interruption resulting from the violent suppression of pro-democracy protesters in and around Tiananmen Square in 1989, the PRC was encouraged in its economic reforms and to enter global society. But as China rose at breakneck speed through the 1980s and 1990s, the suspicion, now mainstream and embedded in PRC political thinking, arose that the US was unwilling to concede its hegemonic position in Asia.

The American security architecture in Asia, notably the US–Japan security alliance, but also various economic policies and strategic ambiguity around the Taiwan issue, are cited by the PRC as evidence of US containment. Taiwan, it is argued, became a tool designed to frustrate PRC development, increase insecurity and thwart national unification. And as "independence" became an openly discussed political position within Taiwan, the PRC saw in US attempts at maintaining equilibrium not a quest for neutrality but a deliberate obstacle to unification.

Viewed through this lens, the PRC can point to examples of "containment" in action. Notably, the US' decision to allow President Lee Teng-hui to visit his alma mater Cornell in an unofficial capacity a year before the first direct election of the ROC president in 1996 prompted a missile crisis in the Taiwan Strait. Subsequent PLA live-fire exercises off the coast of Taiwan prompted President Clinton to dispatch the Pacific-based Seventh Fleet to prevent escalation. This, the PRC interpreted as evidence of the US' true intentions to interfere in Taiwan, to implicitly support independence and to prevent national unification.

In subsequent years the PRC has interpreted, genuinely or instrumentally, any positive interaction the US has with Taiwan as interference or containment. From the PRC's perspective, the US–Taiwan relationship is inherently harmful to China's national interests and it can find in

American policy and rhetoric towards Taiwan ample confirmation of this suspicion. This interpretative lens has become easier with the rise of bipartisan hawkishness towards China, and the genuine or performative enthusiasm many American politicians now display towards supporting Taiwan. This includes some political actors who directly call for the US to enhance or formalize its relationship with Taiwan in order to push back against PRC aggression. Such rhetoric is counterproductive for the US–Taiwan relationship, and feeds the PRC suspicion and narrative that the US is using Taiwan to contain China.

PELOSI AND THE TRAJECTORY OF US–TAIWAN RELATIONS

When Nancy Pelosi led a delegation to Taiwan on 2–3 August 2022, it seemed a watershed moment. Although US–Taiwan relations have become progressively closer over the past few years, the Pelosi visit seemed to catalyse a moment of fundamental change in the US–Taiwan–PRC triangular relationship. It was controversial for a number of reasons. First, as Speaker of the House, she was the highest-level politician to visit Taiwan since Newt Gingrich in the 1990s. But it was not simply her position that made Pelosi's trip controversial, the timing was also significant. US–China relations are in flux, and the direction of the relationship is in question following years of increasing suspicion and antagonism since the latter years of the Obama administration through the abrasive Trump administration and the Covid-19 pandemic. Even before Pelosi's visit, bilateral relations were deteriorating and increasingly conflictual. When Pelosi went to Taiwan it was interpreted in the PRC as rubbing salt in the open wound of US–China relations. The fact that she was an inveterate China critic with a decades-long history of advocacy for human rights and democracy in the PRC, made it all the more irritating for the PRC.

From the Taiwanese government's perspective, the Pelosi visit was welcomed as a signal of enduring American support amid intensifying PRC pressures across diverse policy sectors. In the Tsai administration's interpretation, the visit was within the bounds of unofficial US–Taiwan relations, and framed as the conventional business of a democratically elected official paying a visit to a fellow democracy. Some of Tsai's domestic critics countered that it was unnecessarily provocative, especially given her hard oppositional stance towards the PRC. Similar divisions and arguments were reflected in debates among Taiwan policy experts in the US. Some argued that it was important to show that the US would not back down in the face of increasing Chinese pressures over Taiwan (Focus Taiwan 2022) and that it was an appropriate signal amid a growing list of Chinese actions that undermined the status quo in East Asia.

For other Taiwan experts, the Pelosi visit was seen as an unnecessarily risky move that heightened the potential for military conflict. These experts argued that even though it may have demonstrated symbolic solidarity with Taiwan, it would give the PRC cause to further increase its military threats towards Taiwan (Christensen *et al.* 2022). Indeed, days after the Pelosi trip concluded, the PLA conducted the largest live-fire military drills since the 1996 Taiwan Strait Crisis. Some American analysts regarded the Pelosi trip as providing the PRC with an excuse to raise tensions to this level, and that it not only hurt peace and stability in the Taiwan Strait, but set US–China reconciliation back even further.

Whether or not the Pelosi visit was a net positive or negative, and for whom, remains to be seen. However, the visit and its fallout have prompted concrete changes to the US–Taiwan relationship, and Taiwan has become a highly salient issue in American domestic politics. While some of this salience is manifest only in rhetoric, there have been substantive developments, including further arms sales, military aid and high-level meetings. It also gave renewed urgency to the process to debate around a new and potentially consequential piece of American legislation, the Taiwan Policy Act (TPA), which included controversial symbolic changes like the de facto embassy in the US changing its name from the Taipei Economic and Cultural Representative Office (TECRO) to the Taiwan Economic Cultural Office. Although the TPA had bipartisan support, the controversial provisions eventually did not pass. Instead, a more pragmatic bill called the Taiwan Enhancement Resilience Act (TERA) passed with more substantive and fewer symbolic policies such as increased funding for Taiwanese security and the promotion of Taiwan's participation in international organizations.

Bills that seek to strengthen different aspects of US–Taiwan relations are frequent and normal practice in American politics. Beyond the complex questions of the One-China policy and strategic ambiguity, the US has continued to develop the scope of its engagement with and commitments to Taiwan through these various policies and bills. During the Trump and Biden administrations, numerous bills designed to strengthen unofficial relations with Taiwan were passed unanimously. For example, the Taiwan Travel Act called for more delegations from the US to travel to Taiwan to signify American commitment. Even though bills may be tempered down to include more substantive policies instead of symbolic policies, from the PRC's perspective, no further enhancement of the US–Taiwan relationship is ever acceptable. For example, when the TPA was being debated, Chinese foreign ministry spokesperson Mao Ning said in October 2022, the legislation "seriously breaches the US's commitment to China on the Taiwan question", and if it became law would "cause extremely serious consequences" (Japan Times 2022). The goal of US–Taiwan policy is subsequently to include as much substance as possible while trying to minimize the levels of provocation towards the PRC.

US–TAIWAN POLICY: SUBSTANCE VS SYMBOLISM

The TPA and eventual TERA demonstrate how substance versus symbolism play a major role in writing and passing new US–Taiwan policies. Substantive policies would imply concrete changes for Taiwan, or for Taiwan's relations with the US or internationally. Trade deals, arms sales or advocating for Taiwan's participation in functional multilateral organizations like those pertaining to public health or aviation could be interpreted as substantive policies. Symbolic policies on the other hand might include sending high-level delegations to Taiwan to show solidarity, or changing TECRO's name from "Taipei" to "Taiwan". Both substance and symbolism are important for the US and Taiwan. Symbolic issues are important for Taiwanese resilience and as a demonstration of the solidity of American support.

Symbolic victories, due to their flashy nature, inevitably upset the PRC far more than quieter substantive policies. For some policy analysts, the preference for substance over symbolism is that such policies promote concrete changes for Taiwan. Trade bills, for example, further tie Taiwan economically to other countries, creating more incentives for countries to care and protect Taiwan's position in the world. Yet, substantive victories are often slower and quieter than their symbolic counterparts. From the PRC's perspective, any policy between the US and Taiwan is considered bad since it consolidates Taiwan's current separation or pulls Taiwan further away from the PRC. Hence if the PRC is going to be upset by the US passing any Taiwan-related policy, it is better for Taiwan to gain something concrete from it. But for other experts, symbolic victories are one of the most powerful ways to push back against Chinese coercion.

A singular policy toward Taiwan that optimizes US and Taiwanese interests probably does not exist, and the US is currently trying to decide what the best direction is for its own Taiwan policy. It will continue to be in the US interest to cultivate intense engagement and solid unofficial relations with Taiwan. Yet it must also consider its relations with China. China and the US are competitors and rivals in many spheres, but the collapse of ties, which could occur in the event of conflict over Taiwan, is not in the US' best interest. The US would prefer a world in which it is able to maintain productive relations with both the PRC and Taiwan, but the preference structure on all sides makes this balancing act increasingly difficult.

7

"The most dangerous place in the world"

In the summer of 2021, *The Economist* published a special section on Taiwan with the tagline "the most dangerous place on earth" (*Economist* 2021). Despite the sensational title, it provided a measured and sober account of the potential for militarized superpower conflict in the Taiwan Strait. It was a reasonable line to take, prompted by increasingly fractious Sino-US relations and deeply frozen cross-Strait relations. It also reflected a long history of academic and policy assessments that have dealt with the same question. Some scholarly research came to a similar conclusion that Taiwan is increasingly in danger, while other work did not and instead see Taiwan's position as still stable (*Foreign Affairs* 2022).

Those with an interest in international relations (IR) theory might be familiar with seeing Taiwan portrayed using different analytical lenses. For example, scholars working within the neorealist approach to IR, which foregrounds power, self-interest and maximization, have tended to see the Taiwan issue as a likely if not inevitable *casus belli* between the US and China. Neorealists explain the absence, to date, of such a confrontation by invoking deterrence. In the case of Taiwan, deterrence has come primarily in the form of American strategic ambiguity backed by the US' superior military capabilities.

Scholars in the neoliberal tradition have been more sanguine about the likelihood of conflict. These scholars foreground trilateral economic interactions and emphasize the stability conferred by the economic institutions and policy architecture constitutive of both US–China and cross-Strait relations. The high costs and disruption that would result from militarized conflict are so daunting that all sides are compelled to avoid actions that would lead to confrontation. These scholars point to the intensification of market connections among the three sides and the economic complementarities that benefit each actor and conclude that there is too much to lose by engaging in war.

Constructivist scholars, with their focus on identity and values, veer between optimistic arguments about common ethnic and cultural bonds on either side of the Strait, and pessimistic observations of the rise of nationalism, competing identities, and values supercharged by diverging national and cultural identities in Taiwan and China. Identity and its ubiquitous presence in domestic and international cross-Strait politics could either be the factor that pushes relations together, or further pulls them apart.

While IR theory is a useful starting point, no metatheoretical approach, or single mid-range theory, has produced a definitive account or framework that can fully encompass the complexities and intractable dimensions of the Taiwan issue (Wu 2000). *The Economist*'s special section was not concerned with the intricacies of academic theorizing, but it encapsulated a general feeling of negative momentum in US–China relations, the intractable nature of positions adopted by the PRC and Taiwan, and the intense militarization of the Taiwan Strait. The PLA's modernization programme over the past two decades has resulted in vastly greater capacity generally and in terms of the specific needs of a hypothetical action in the Taiwan Strait. The substantial military advantage that the US once enjoyed has narrowed, possibly to a point approaching parity.

The PRC has never renounced the use of force with regard to Taiwan, but for decades the PRC position has been to pursue "peaceful unification" while only reserving the threat of military action to prevent "Taiwan independence". As we discussed in Chapter 4, Taiwan's democratic leaders have rejected "Taiwan independence", thereby upholding the status quo that is key to maintaining international support. However, by consolidating de facto independence and prolonging separation from the PRC, Taiwan has frustrated the PRC's hopes for progress towards unification. The PRC has responded by exerting increasing pressure on Taiwan and seemingly stretching the definition of independence to include the exercise of the ROC's existing autonomy. This has been framed in the West as PRC revisionism and determination to alter the status quo. In this scenario, strategic calculations and the risk of conflict in the Strait will diverge significantly from the preceding four decades.

Such a prospect has become all the more salient after Russia's invasion of Ukraine in February 2022. Although the two theatres are not analogous (see Templeman 2021 for disambiguation), it stimulated in Taiwan an official and popular response that speaks to Taiwan's vulnerabilities and the seriousness of the PRC threat. Taiwan's response to Ukraine and the PRC's post-Pelosi live-fire drills was measured and focused on appropriate policy responses. Instead of mass panic, runs on the stock market or mass emigration, Taiwanese people remained calm. This sanguinity has surprised many foreign visitors to Taiwan. When *The Economist* issue came out it prompted an outpouring of Taiwanese posts online showing examples of people going about their normal business amid peaceful and comfortable lifestyles. Taiwan has faced military threats from the PRC for many decades, and Taiwanese people have shown that they are not easily cowed. Threats and intimidation have invariably been met with composure, determination and a refusal to be coerced.

CHINESE MILITARY THREATS UNDER XI JINPING

PRC pressures directed at Taiwan are not new to Xi Jinping's tenure. The threat of militarized conflict is also longstanding (Lieberthal 2005). As noted in previous chapters, until American intervention at the outset of China's involvement in the Korean War in 1950, it looked likely that the PLA would invade Taiwan. Subsequent missile crises in the 1950s and in 1995–96 were a reminder of the PRC's ability, motivation and willingness to employ military means (Scobell 2000). They also highlighted the immutable fact of Taiwan's proximity to the PRC. In places, it is a mere 130 km across the Strait from the PRC to the main island of Taiwan. The ROC-held islands of Kinmen and Matsu, populated by more than 100,000 Taiwanese citizens, are much closer than that. Kinmen is barely 10 km from the Chinese city of Xiamen on the coast of Fujian Province. These small outlying islands are especially vulnerable, being almost impossible to defend should the PLA decide to advance on them. They represent a possible preliminary or escalatory target for hypothetical military scenarios. The sense of vulnerability is reflected in the voting behaviour of these areas, which invariably favours the KMT.

Between the 1995–96 missile crisis and the live-fire drills in response to Speaker Pelosi's visit in 2022, the PRC largely refrained from demonstrations of military might directed at Taiwan. In recent years, that has changed, with the routinization of PLAAF jets entering Taiwan's Air Defence Identification Zone (ADIZ). However, these exercises, intended to test the Taiwanese military and intimidate Taiwanese people, did not rise to the level of actual military action. One reason for the relative quiet during this period was the backlash that the 1995–96 episode generated in Taiwan. The PLA missiles were intended to cow Taiwanese voters in the first presidential election. They were expected to persuade Taiwanese voters to reject Lee Teng-hui and choose instead the PRC's preferred pro-unification candidates. Lee won in a landslide, and the threat was great enough that the US dispatched the US Seventh Fleet to patrol the neighbouring seas.

This was a learning moment for the PRC, but it is uncertain what lesson was learned. Was it that attempting to influence the outcome of Taiwanese elections through threatening behaviour did not work? Or was it the realization that the PLA was simply not powerful enough for the threats to have the intended effect? Either way, subsequent Taiwanese elections were not subject to similar military intimidation, while resources were diverted into quieter and less overt "influence activities" and substantial investment in preparing for potential military contingencies.

The PLA's capacity building and modernization has proceeded at stunning speed, with particular advances in its preparedness for kinetic action in the Taiwan Strait theatre. A major shake-up of the PLA in 2015 saw a reorganization of military command structures and services, overseen by Xi Jinping (Wuthnow & Saunders 2017). These reforms were designed, in large part, to facilitate the needs of a potential military action against Taiwan. The Eastern Theatre Command in particular has been reorganized and equipped with a military operation against Taiwan and potential interventions by the US and Japan in mind. The result of the PLA's patient preparations is that the Strait is more highly militarized and the balance of power is more equal than at any previous time.

The US State Department predicts that on the current trajectory the military balance will tilt in the PRC's favour by 2027 (Demirjian 2022). This would be a significant landmark, indicating that PRC military action to defeat and take Taiwan would become a political option for the CCP regime. It does not mean that the PLA would be able to take Taiwan easily or that the consequences of an attack or invasion would be negligible, or even tolerable, for the PRC leadership. Critically, capabilities and intent are not synonymous; just because the PRC is able to attack Taiwan does not mean it necessarily will. But it means that the strategic calculus moves from refraining from military action due to inferior forces to the political will to start and engage in an attack.

The opacity that surrounds PRC policymaking makes it difficult to discern the strategic decision making and contingency planning conversations at the highest levels. But what is clear is that Xi has tied his own legitimacy and that of the CCP to "rejuvenation of the Chinese nation" and "national unification" is integral to the project. It also has an ostensible deadline: 2049. If progress towards a "voluntary" unification process is not made, and if Taiwan's de facto independence is further consolidated domestically and receives tacit support internationally, initiating the PLA option will increase in likelihood.

The preceding few years under Xi give a flavour of the PRC's capabilities and willingness to ramp up its capabilities while still pledging support for peaceful development and peaceful unification. Over this period, the PLA has registered a number of "firsts": the first circumnavigation of Taiwan in 2016; the first nocturnal sorties in 2018; the first intrusion by PLAAF jets across the median line of the Taiwan Strait in 2020. Earlier "firsts", like incursions into Taiwan's ADIZ and aircraft carrier sail throughs of the Taiwan Strait have already become routine. The military exercises rolled out after Speaker Pelosi's visit gave an indication of what an escalation of military intimidation might look like, with PLA air and naval forces operating close to Taiwan and encircling the island in what amounted to a blockade (Zhao 2022). Missiles were also fired over the island into the Pacific Ocean, including at high altitude across the capital city, Taipei. The speed with which these forces were mobilized, and the precision and smoothness with which the exercises were carried out, suggests long planning and preparedness.

THE RISE OF HYBRID WARFARE

The potential for conflict in the Strait, always latent but often masked, is due to irreconcilable preferences, an increasingly equal military balance and high stakes for all sides. In recent years, China and the US have increased their deterrence while decreasing their acts of reassurance, thus threatening the delicate equilibrium that prevailed for many years (Zuo 2021). With increasing military firepower and activity in the region, the opportunity for miscalculation or accidents has increased. The decline in mutual trust, communication channels and crisis management mechanisms among the three sides increase the chances of a collision or incident involving military forces escalating, or even spiralling out of control. Meanwhile, non-kinetic hybrid modes of warfare like cyber, information and psychological warfare have become increasingly routine. Although military threats are the fundamental means through which the PRC tries to influence Taiwan, it is only one of many domains in which the PRC seeks to coerce Taiwanese behaviour and attitudes.

Economic coercion has also been a prime strategy for the PRC. The PRC's opening to Taiwanese capital and business was conceived as a mechanism that would bind the two economies and create the conditions and motivation for unification. Economic interaction has not had the PRC's desired spillover effect. It has not established overwhelming leverage over the Taiwanese economy nor has it made Taiwanese business interests a force for unification. The PRC has never been coy about using its economic power and the attraction of the Chinese market for political ends. As its ambitions for unification have been frustrated, the connection between politics and economics has become manifest in punitive actions against Taiwan. Taiwanese firms that are seen to favour "independence" or the "DPP separatists" have been subject to informal sanctions, market access bans and consumer boycotts (Wu 2021). During Tsai's tenure even companies with outspoken opposition to independence have been collateral damage when the CCP wants to signal its displeasure (Ellis & Chang 2021). Taiwanese producers, farmers and fishers have been subject to sudden bans on exporting goods to the PRC (Hioe 2022). Refusals to import agricultural produce like pineapples or grouper fish on the basis of enhanced health and quality inspections at convenient political junctures, are especially designed to hit DPP-supporting constituencies in the rural south and east of Taiwan. They have generally failed since Taiwanese and international consumers, in solidarity, have taken up the slack (Ko 2021). "Made in Taiwan" imports that fail to explicitly state that Taiwan is part of China have been scrutinized and destroyed (Cheng & Li 2022). Exports of raw materials and resources like sand to Taiwan have been arbitrarily halted (Liu 2022). Limits have been placed on the number of PRC tourists and overseas students allowed to travel to Taiwan in a bid to harm those sectors (Ihara 2019).

Meanwhile, Taiwanese businesspeople in the PRC have faced an increasingly difficult and hostile environment, with little hope of Taiwanese or international institutional support. Taiwanese entertainers operating in the lucrative Chinese market have been persuaded to express support for PRC positions toward Taiwan (Kim 2019), and Taiwanese NGO workers have been detained and jailed for activities that purportedly "endanger national security" or promote "secession" (Pan 2021). Evidence for such crimes can be as tenuous as having connections to the DPP. Members of the DPP have experienced increasing limits to their access to China and Hong Kong, and sitting government officials have been sanctioned and banned for "diehard independence" attitudes (Tian & Blanchard 2022).

Some of the PRC's behaviours can appear petty or abstruse, but the policy context behind them is explicable from the PRC perspective (Brown 2020). There are numerous examples where the PRC has used its economic and diplomatic leverage to freeze Taiwan out of international participation, even where statehood is not a requirement. For many Taiwanese people international participation is an indicator of "national dignity", which has been a sore spot for many decades. Taiwanese people rightly believe that Taiwan's achievements of economic modernization and democratization have not been rewarded with a commensurate international role. For the PRC, cognisant of this frustration and yearning on the part of Taiwanese people, denying international participation and "poaching" the ROC's diplomatic allies are levers to delegitimize the Taiwanese government (Shattuck 2020). It is also another way to exert psychological pressure, sending a message to Taiwanese people that the only path to "dignity" is via unification. The PRC's intense pressure on

Taiwan in the international sphere is partly related to its manifold operations in the psychological domain.

Information, cognitive, psychological and cyber-warfare operations have intensified significantly under Xi Jinping (Harold *et al.* 2021). These activities are not necessarily about convincing Taiwanese people to support the PRC. Instead, they are often designed to undermine Taiwan's government and demoralize Taiwanese people. Propaganda operations aim to convince Taiwanese people that the future is bleak and that unification is inevitable. Disinformation efforts attack the legitimacy of Taiwan's democratic institutions and seek to exacerbate social divisions. Largely unsuccessful efforts have been made to co-opt Taiwanese elites, influence Taiwanese media, and stir up trouble through connections to local crime organizations. Officers in the Taiwanese military have been flipped to create the impression that it is compromised and unable to defend Taiwan's interests. These are just some of the deliberate efforts by various Chinese state actors to make Taiwanese people feel that resistance to unification is futile and that access to respect, prosperity and security is only possible under the auspices of "one country, two systems".

TAIWAN'S EFFORTS TO DEFEND ITSELF

We have shown in Chapter 3 that the mainstream preference in Taiwan is to maintain de facto independence as the ROC and to resist attempts by the PRC to coerce Taiwan into accepting unification under duress. This posture requires Taiwan to prepare for potential actions by the PLA. The current consensus in Taiwanese defence circles is that Taiwan must be able and willing to defend itself. This may sound obvious, but one criticism levelled against Taiwanese governments, by the US, is that Taiwan has been complacent, overly sanguine about the probability of a military attack and too reliant on the prospect of American military intervention. Consequently, for many years Taiwanese defence spending was incommensurate with the level of threat presented by the PRC.

Taiwan's military preparedness has suffered numerous challenges. In terms of personnel it has faced consistent shortfalls in reservists, limited combat training for conscripts and political obstacles to moving to a professional all-volunteer force. In terms of equipment, a previous policy of developing a symmetric response led to the acquisition of prestige platforms with less utility for the purpose they need to serve. There have also been issues with obsolescence, ageing and maintenance, manifest in numerous military training accidents. Taiwan's defence strategy, as the US has encouraged for several years, now embraces an asymmetric force as the best option for responding to a PRC attack. Taiwanese forces, even with American weapons and assistance, cannot hope to out muscle the PLA, but it can delay PLA advances and increase the PRC's risk. The realization that an asymmetrical defence strategy is Taiwan's best option has been refined and encapsulated by the term "porcupine strategy". Although the specifics of defence policy are subject to intense political debates in Taiwan, there is increasing recognition that over-reliance on outside help is not an optimal strategy either.

In Tsai Ing-wen's second inauguration speech in 2020, she emphasized the need for military reform. Since then, she has increased Taiwan's military budget for arms purchases, openly accepts American military aid and expanded training and information sharing. Under Tsai there is a willingness in Taiwan's government to foreground Taiwanese self-defence, which was not characteristic of her immediate predecessors. It is evident in substantial defence budget increases, speeding up reforms to military service and even the increasing reverence with which Tsai talks about the military. In 2022, Tsai extended military conscription from four months to one year, a move lauded by all political parties in Taiwan. Although Taiwan has been slow to act on defence spending in the past, that has changed under Tsai although other critical defence policy reforms still have a long way to go.

In addition to a new focus on preparing to defend itself, Taiwan under Tsai Ing-wen has actively sought international support and had done so in a global strategic context. Tsai has emphasized Taiwan's contribution to the global economy and its position on the frontline of a global contest between democracy and authoritarianism. Contrary to descriptions of Taiwan as "small", and compared to the PRC it is, the Taiwanese landmass is not insignificant by global standards. Neither is Taiwan's population of 24 million people, which places it 57th in the world. By any standard, Taiwan is a high achiever in terms of economic, technological and social development. Its transition to a consolidated liberal democracy is a beacon in Asia. A PRC attack on Taiwan would therefore have major implications for global democracy and bring significant disruption to the world economy, especially given the dominant global role of the Taiwanese semiconductor industry, which we shall discuss in Chapter 8. The West's preference for a "rules-based international order" and a "free and open Indo-Pacific" would be severely damaged. This explains why the threat to Taiwan's autonomy, and Taiwan's determination to resist PRC coercion, has become so resonant in many western countries.

Taiwanese civil society is also aware of the increasingly turbulent Taiwan Strait. When Nancy Pelosi visited Taiwan, reports of Taiwanese responses to the PRC's military threats were seen as muted. Unlike many of the headlines in the western world that described the military drills as a "Fourth Strait Crisis", Taiwanese were notably measured in response. Taiwanese however, are not unaware of PRC threats or immune to the likelihood of war, but they have become a routine backdrop to life in Taiwan. Rather than eliciting a dramatic response, Taiwanese people, institutions and society have developed the resilience to quietly carry on despite the increased frequency and intensity of PRC threats. This seemingly imperturbable attitude has come in for criticism in Taiwan, lest it give way to complacency. It has provoked some outside criticism too, where it is misdiagnosed as nonchalance. For instance, one survey conducted in 2021 showed that 57 per cent of Taiwanese citizens worry about a possible war in the Strait and keenly felt a qualitative and quantitative change in PRC threats against Taiwan (Rigger *et al.* 2021).

INTERNATIONALIZATION OF SECURITY IN THE TAIWAN STRAIT

A PRC-held Taiwan would fundamentally change the security and strategic situation in the Western Pacific. As an "unsinkable aircraft carrier" Taiwan would give the PLA control of the first island chain and the capacity to project its power far from the Chinese coast into the Pacific. For the PRC, controlling Taiwan would allow the country to break through American "containment", increasing Chinese security and weakening American alliance structures in China's immediate vicinity. For a corollary set of reasons, it would threaten the interests not just of the US, but Japan, Australia and other regional actors concerned about China's intentions. The existing US security architecture, including security alliances with Japan and Korea, would be severely challenged. The US and its democratic allies in the region thus assess Taiwan's defence and security from the perspective of strategic self-interest as much as shared values and norms. The US' willingness to sell increasingly sophisticated "defensive weapons" to Taiwan should be interpreted in this light. At this juncture, it seems likely that a PRC attack on Taiwan would prompt American intervention on Taiwan's behalf, but it is not only Taiwan and the US that are preparing for such a contingency.

Numerous countries have signalled concern and contingency planning for a potential conflict in the Taiwan Strait. One such country is Japan, a major regional player and key US defence ally. Japan's relations with China are characterized by mutual suspicion and historical legacies, but also intense trade and investment relations. In recent years Japan has evinced concerns about unilateral attempts to change the status quo by the use of force in the Indo-Pacific, clearly indicating the PRC and Taiwan. In response, the Japanese government has launched a new National Security Strategy and Defence Build-up Plan, which sets out steps to transform the capabilities of Japan's Self-Defence Forces. This paradigm shift will require significant changes to Japan's defence acquisition strategy and a radical overhaul of its defence industrial base.

Japan's National Security Strategy portrays "some nations", presumably Russia and China, that are "guided by their own historical views and values, not sharing universal values, [that] are making attempts to revise the existing international order". This authoritarian revisionism Japan says has made the challenges to its security environment more "severe and complex" than ever. To address such concerns Japan's main priorities are to develop its own national defence capacities and to coordinate with the US. The two sides have discussed, for example, expanding cooperation in numerous mission areas and enhancing employment of Japan's counterstrike capabilities. Whether such capabilities could be part of a US response to hypothetical conflict in the Taiwan Strait – unthinkable until very recently – is up for political debate in Japan.

Japan has a further evolving strategy of building a multi-layered network of allied and like-minded countries. In 2022, it signed a Reciprocal Access Agreement (RAA) with Australia, followed by a comprehensive bilateral security agreement covering cooperation in the military, intelligence and cybersecurity sectors. A year later, Japan signed an RAA with the UK, which builds on existing bilateral cooperation in the security technology sector and will facilitate joint training, exercises and potentially operations.

These agreements are symptomatic of a new networked framework of defence cooperation among American allies, arrived at independently and unmediated by the US. Although not explicitly or solely focused on the Taiwan Strait, there are clear signs that US allies are making moves to counter what they claim to be the Chinese threat to the status quo and international order, of which Taiwan is the clearest symbol. The US is also keen to involve other partners in enhancing security in the region, as illustrated by the new AUKUS security agreement with Australia and the UK to produce nuclear-powered submarines over the coming two decades. Expanding the membership of existing US and regional democratic partner cooperations, such as the Five Eyes intelligence sharing agreement and the Quadrilateral Security Dialogue, is another likely development.

From the PRC perspective, these developments further complicate China's strategic situation and objectives regarding the pursuit of national unification. For all the PRC's proclamations that Taiwan is an internal Chinese affair, the Taiwan issue is becoming increasingly internationalized and contingency planners in the PRC must now consider the likelihood of a multinational military response to a hypothetical PLA action against Taiwan.

OUTSIDE ACTORS: EUROPE AND THE UK

In many western democracies the deterioration of bilateral relations with the PRC, prompted by a perception of the PRC as an authoritarian actor intent on revising the status quo, have sharpened views on supporting Taiwan to defend itself and resist coercion. This trend has intensified since Russia's invasion of Ukraine, with numerous countries outside the region showing greater interest in Taiwan. The European Union (EU) and various European nations have followed the US in publishing their own Indo-Pacific strategies. A succession of parliamentary delegations has visited Taiwan in the past few years, from the EU, UK, Canada and other western nations. The succession of western visitors to Taiwan symbolizes the progressive internationalization of the Taiwan issue, something that Taiwan's government has been keen to nurture. The UK is a good example of an outside actor that has developed a keen interest in what happens in the Taiwan Strait and how it affects the broader region.

For 50 years the UK's "One-China policy" has been the foundation of Sino-UK relations. Every UK government in this period has accepted that productive relations with the PRC were predicated on upholding it. However, the coda to the UK's acknowledgement of the PRC's claim over Taiwan is that any resolution to the Taiwan issue should be arrived at peacefully through "constructive dialogue" and any changes to the status quo should reflect the preferences of people on both sides of the Strait. The UK thus opposes any unilateral change in the Taiwan Strait, whether in the form of "Taiwan independence" or through coerced unification or military aggression.

Taiwan has not traditionally been a salient issue in British politics. Taiwan is far away, with limited historical connections. Annual UK–Taiwan trade talks have been ongoing for two decades, but despite some complementarities and potential for growth in various sectors, UK exports of goods and services to Taiwan reached £2.4 billion, good for 39th place among the UK's trade partners in 2020. Imports from Taiwan in 2020 reached £3.6 billion, accounting for just 0.7 per cent of UK imports. Despite the lack of connections, the salience of Taiwan has increased substantially along with bipartisan political support and sympathy for Taiwan's predicament. The general deterioration of UK–China relations and anger over Hong Kong's National Security Law have coincided with the ambitions of a post-Brexit "Global Britain" and "Indo-Pacific tilt". The UK has identified support for the continuation of Taiwan's de facto separation as integral to the concept and practice of a "free and open Indo-Pacific".

A delegation of MPs from the House of Commons' influential Foreign Affairs Committee visited Taiwan in 2023, the first such visit for 16 years. Committee chair Alicia Kearns MP described her hosts as one of "the strongest democracies on Earth" and a "steadfast friend". She called for Taiwan's participation and full membership of multilateral bodies like the World Health Organization and an end to the "unjust obstructionism" that prevents Taiwan from joining. Just a fortnight earlier, another

British government delegation, led by the Minister for International Trade Greg Hands, was in Taiwan for bilateral trade talks. On the sidelines of the G-20 summit in Bali in 2022 Prime Minister Rishi Sunak refused to rule out sending arms to Taiwan and declared that "we stand ready to support Taiwan, as we do in standing up to Chinese aggression". Rhetoric like this, unthinkable in even the recent past, has become normal in UK politics.

What the UK would be able or willing to contribute in the event of military conflict in the Taiwan Strait is debatable. The Royal Navy's HMS *Queen Elizabeth* carrier group sailed through the Taiwan Strait in 2021, and the RAA with Japan makes a sustainable naval presence more feasible. However, the broader relevance of the UK's interest in East Asian security is that it would work closely with the US, and regional partners like Japan and Australia, to support a coordinated American-led response to potential conflict. The UK already has close security cooperation with the US, and is looking to increase coordination with Japan, Australia and India. The expansion of the UK's bilateral and multilateral cooperation has been welcomed by the US. For the first time, in 2022, the two sides held a high-level meeting to discuss plans for cooperation and contingencies related to Taiwan. The new Taiwan Dialogue mechanism is symptomatic of a deliberate US effort to expand the coalition of countries willing to get involved in the Taiwan issue. For the UK, Taiwan has emerged as a place of strategic importance, central to challenges to the "rules-based international order", maintenance of the "free and open Indo-Pacific" project and connecting Euro-Atlantic and Indo-Pacific security together.

CONFLICT SCENARIOS, STRATEGIES AND PROBABILITIES

A longstanding but increasingly urgent question in academic and policy circles is what conflict over Taiwan might look like, and how best to respond (Tsang 2006). The assumption is that any conflict would be initiated by the PRC, and therefore the PLA would enjoy first-mover advantage. However, the military materiel and troop movements required for a large-scale attack, let alone full invasion, would be substantial and hard to conceal. Taiwan and its allies can then count on some sort of head-start in rolling out its response. Taiwanese intelligence gathering, added to routine operations of the US and Japan, is highly attuned to PLA preparations. Taiwan does not face credible threats to its security apart from the PRC, so the Taiwanese military is able to concentrate its attention and resources on potential PLA operations.

The first issue to assess is the scale and nature of a PLA operation against Taiwan. Scenario planners in Taipei have responses for diverse contingencies, ranging from concerted misinformation and propaganda efforts, cyber-attacks, naval blockade, missile attacks and bombing of military installations and infrastructure, to a full-scale amphibious assault with landing troops. The repertoire available to the PLA facilitates both incremental escalation and a multi-pronged attack. Taiwan is already subject to misinformation, propaganda and cyber-attacks, and the PLA's live-fire drills in August 2022 amounted to a temporary and bounded blockade, encircling the island of Taiwan and preventing the normal operation of Taiwanese sea and airports.

Planners in Taiwan and the US expect the PRC to escalate incrementally, rather than mount a sudden and unsignalled invasion. This could involve cyber-attacks on critical infrastructure, intensification of air and naval force activity across the median line and around the island, and actions to take ROC-claimed uninhabited islands in the South China Sea. More serious would be potential actions against ROC-held Kinmen and Matsu off the coast of Fujian. While the Taiwanese military has defence capacity on these two small but inhabited islands, their proximity to the PRC makes them largely impossible to defend against a determined antagonist. The political question is how determined the ROC would be to try to retain control of Kinmen and Matsu, and whether the US and other regional allies would interpret such a move as an attack on Taiwan. It is likely that such a move would result in international sanctions against the PRC, but not an American military response.

PRC success in taking Kinmen or Matsu would be framed in the PRC as proof of its military prowess, its courage to stand up to American intimidation and evidence of the regime's determination to prevent "independence" and further the goal of national reunification. However, it would also unite western countries against the PRC and depending on the scale of sanctions could be highly disruptive. However, the PRC may determine that it is worth the risk, having seen Russia ride out severe sanctions following the invasion of Ukraine. The difference is that Russia could call on China for economic support, whereas China is much more embedded and therefore vulnerable to the global economy. In any case, it is unlikely that having established national unification as a core regime goal, that taking Kinmen and Matsu would satisfy the PLA's ambitions. The danger of taking these islands as a precursor to mounting an attack on Taiwan proper is that it would signal their intentions and allow Taiwan and potential allies to prepare a response, no doubt including dispatch of the US Seventh Fleet and other materiel located in Japan and the Western Pacific.

The motivation of a PRC attack on Taiwan would be to take control of the island, pacify resistance and initiate processes by which the PRC could formally exert its rule. Large-scale destruction of Taiwan with missiles would defeat the PRC's purpose, which is to absorb it into PRC rule under "one country, two systems". Therefore, any invasion would require an amphibious assault and the dispatch of land troops to quell what is likely to be highly motivated and sustained Taiwanese resistance, plus likely American involvement. This necessity makes a Chinese attack complex and risky, with numerous points at which Taiwanese (and/or US) forces could disrupt it. The Taiwan Strait itself represents a formidable obstacle to amphibious invasion. Conditions in the Strait are unsuited to landing waterborne forces for all but a few months of the year, and the beaches of Taiwan's west coast are amenable to patrolling and defending. An invasion is thus the riskiest and presently least likely scenario.

THE UTILITY OF DELAYED GRATIFICATION

One counter-intuitive idea is that unfulfilled "reunification" of Taiwan is actually politically useful for the CCP. The promise of a soon-to-be-fulfilled goal that is always just out of reach due to the anti-China machinations of traitorous secessionists in Taiwan and a hostile US is a useful way to coalesce regime supportive popular nationalism. The CCP can argue that fulfilment of the dream of national unification and the rejuvenation of the Chinese nation it would symbolize will only be achieved through the regime, which therefore should be supported in its management of the country. This kind of argument, using the US as foil, has been made in other contexts of "China's rise". It justifies increasing expenditure on the military and nurtures patriotic or nationalistic feelings that can then be used to demonstrate to Taiwan and others the strength of popular support behind the unification project. Most usefully of all, the issue can be invoked at politically convenient moments when the regime is in need of an issue on which there is unified domestic support.

This instrumental reading is not totally convincing, and it is not to suggest that the long-term goal of unification is simply a tactic to divert attention from other issues. Moreover, the PRC view that the US does not want to see Taiwan folded into the PRC for its own strategic interests is correct. However, let us reformulate these considerations in a different way. Supposing an attack was successful to the extent that PRC troops land on Taiwan, what then? Taiwan is motivated and capable, and any attempt at occupation would likely involve sustained Taiwanese military and civilian resistance requiring huge PRC resources and dragging the PRC into the kind of messy occupation that it derided the US for in Iraq and Afghanistan.[1] Quelling Taiwanese forces would likely result in the mass destruction of Taiwanese infrastructure and society, requiring huge investment to rebuild. The value of a physically destroyed Taiwan, a long and painful occupation, and the economic pain caused by severe and enduring international sanctions is substantially lower than peaceful unification. And perhaps of having reunification as a unifying incentive for Chinese society to work towards.

One potential way to keep the peace that some political scientists have argued is the role of trade. If Taiwan and the PRC's economies are deeply interdependent, embedded in the global economy and enmeshed in relevant institutional frameworks that might deter conflict by raising the costs. However, even accepting that economic relations might serve as a deterrent does not make them straightforward or apolitical. On the contrary, economic issues in Taiwan are highly politicized, as we discuss in the next chapter.

---

1. While we do not know for certain how Ukraine has changed Xi's thinking towards Taiwan, Russia's invasion of Ukraine is also likely to influence how the PRC thinks about invasion and the potential global response to its action.

113

8

Taiwan's political economy

In the decades following the Second World War Taiwan transitioned to a newly industrialized country (NIC) and became one of four "Asian Tigers" with Singapore, South Korea and Hong Kong. The rapid and sustained growth experienced by these economies has been the subject of decades of political economy research. The puzzle has been to explain how they successfully transitioned from low-performing economies to integral parts of the global economic order, unlike many developing economies. One of the development strategies used to achieve this result was export-oriented industrialization. Prior to the Asian Tigers' success, economists were sceptical of export-oriented industrialization. Yet, Taiwan made it work.

The conditions for rapid development were not immediately favourable. Taiwan in the early 1950s was in a chaotic state. The KMT was engaged in a brutal crackdown on local Taiwanese through the White Terror and martial law. Chiang Kai-shek was preoccupied with the prospect of war with the PRC, leading to disproportionate spending on the military and defence. Hyperinflation and instability were rampant, and the KMT desperately needed to stabilize the economy *and* find an economic plan that would lead to growth. Economic reform was needed, but priorities were unfocused. The KMT leadership was made up of officials with backgrounds in the military or engineering, most of whom had minimal economic policy experience. The authoritarian KMT was amenable to a strong interventionist state with the government operating state-owned enterprises (SOEs), but was largely uninterested in developing the private sector. The ROC was also heavily reliant on US aid, which was largely keeping Taiwan's economy afloat.

From 1957, when the US began cutting back its aid to Taiwan, the KMT realized that reform was urgently needed. It pushed the KMT to prioritize economic and party reform in order to reduce its dependency on the US. Economists and bureaucratic planners would have a bigger say in how to grow Taiwan's economy. A combination of Taiwanese bureaucrats from the KMT and the International Monetary Fund (IMF) began collaborating on ideas to overcome Taiwan's economic problems. They agreed that Taiwan's reliance on the American foreign exchange was its biggest problem, and that it was not taking full advantage of its potential to export. Together, these technocrats devised a plan to simplify foreign exchange rates and devalue the New Taiwan Dollar so that Taiwanese goods would be much more competitive on the international market. Soon after these policy changes were introduced exports began to soar. Export industries were liberalized, attracting foreign direct investment (FDI) into Taiwan and incentivizing local manufacturing firms. The KMT also began supporting the industries that they thought most likely to succeed, notably plastics and electronics.

State-controlled liberalization defined Taiwan's economic growth for the next several decades. The KMT would selectively intervene in certain industries or enterprises, often in response to economic problems or political incentives. Scholars have debated the extent to which Taiwan's economic growth was due to the KMT's light-touch approach to critical industries and support for free-market export economics. Others argue that it was actually the KMT government's intervention and state support for certain industries that led to Taiwan's economic success. Ironically, both market economists and planned economists consider Taiwan to be an example of the success of their respective models.

Unlike Japan or Korea, where key industries were designed and run by a small group of families or businesses, most of Taiwan's companies were small- to medium-sized enterprises (SMEs) and widely dispersed around Taiwan. Having many firms that could produce and export goods instead of a select few major conglomerates distinguishes Taiwan's experience from other Asian Tigers. Liberalized export sectors became the primary driver of Taiwanese growth, but much of the rest of Taiwan's economy was not liberalized and faced heavy restrictions from the state. In other words, the KMT was careful about which parts of the economy it liberalized while keeping much of the economy under its control.

THE POLITICS OF TRADE

Reaping the benefits of its development model, Taiwan became a large, diversified and globally embedded economy. In 2021 Taiwan was the 22nd largest economy in the world by nominal GDP. It was the 18th largest economy by purchasing power parity and the 8th largest in Asia. China is Taiwan's largest trading partner. In 2021 it accounted for 25 per cent of Taiwan's total trade (Cheng 2022). The US is Taiwan's second largest trading partner accounting for 12 per cent of Taiwan's total trade in 2021 (US Trade Representative 2022). Broken down further, China and Hong Kong accounted for 42 per cent of Taiwan's exports, whereas the United States came in at 15 per cent. Both numbers are growing. Between 2016 and 2021, Taiwanese exports to China grew by 71 per cent, and exports to the US increased by 97 per cent. Meanwhile, Taiwan's imports from China grew by 87 per cent over the period 2017–22 versus 44 per cent growth from the US.

The global significance of Taiwan's economy does not absolve it from its complicated political situation. Yet, neither China's claim over Taiwan nor Sino-US competition has prevented intense economic relations among all sides. Even under President Tsai Ing-wen, who's DPP administration was denied any formal diplomatic channels to the PRC, China was a major source of Taiwanese economic growth. Put another way, the PRC demonstrated an openness to expanding economic ties with Taiwan, even while refusing to deal with the president and party that was in power. Within Taiwan, economic cooperation with the PRC has long been a political issue. It was not until the 1990s that trade and investment was allowed at all, and direct communication links were not fully opened until the 2000s. Even now, many sectors remain off limits to PRC investment and the Taiwan government places restrictions on Taiwanese companies seeking to do business in China. Fears that business links would "hollow out" Taiwanese industry or increase Taiwan's vulnerability by ceding economic leverage to the PRC have been salient and politically contested for three decades.

Despite uneasy political relations, economic interactions across the Strait rapidly expanded in the decades after Chinese leader Deng Xiaoping launched his reform and opening up policies. When President Chiang Ching-kuo lifted the decades-long ban on Taiwanese people travelling to China in 1987, Taiwanese businesses immediately began scouting for investment opportunities. During the 1980s the cost of manufacturing in Taiwan had significantly increased, due to land and labour costs and stricter industry and environmental standards, which made China an attractive alternative. Many Taiwanese businesspeople saw the newly opened Chinese market as a place to replicate their domestic successes with cheap production for export markets. When Taiwan lifted the ban on investing in China in 1992, Taiwan–China economic relations went into overdrive. Unlike other sources of FDI, Taiwanese capital enjoyed preferential treatment in the PRC. This was a political choice, since the PRC hoped that trade and development on China's Southeastern coast would incentivize economic cooperation and ultimately promote unification with Taiwan. It was also extremely lucrative for Taiwanese business-people who were feeling the economic slowdown in Taiwan in the 1980s and 1990s. In her book *The Tiger Leading the Dragon*, Shelley Rigger traces the emergence of a symbiotic relationship between Taiwanese and PRC actors in the 1990s, and identifies Taiwanese investment as a key factor in China's economic take-off (Rigger 2021).

Trade between the two sides reached a climax under Taiwan's Pres-ident Ma Ying-jeou. Before Ma's tenure, beginning in 2008, there were no direct flights between Taiwan and China, and the lack of direct trans-port links was an obstacle to both commercial travel and shipping goods across the Strait. By the time he stood down in 2016, Ma had overseen the liberalization of communication links and concluded 23 economic agreements. As an opposition party in the years before his presidency began, Ma's KMT had agreed in principle to a number of accords with the CCP. More willing and able than the DPP to work with the CCP and accommodate the PRC's requirement to publicly acknowledge the concept of One China, KMT leaders visited China in 2005 during the presidency of the DPP's Chen Shui-bian. This unofficial tour marked the first time that KMT leaders had met their CCP counterparts in China since the Civil War. Not endorsed by the actual Taiwanese government, leading KMT politicians undertook several subsequent missions to meet with PRC government and CCP officials to discuss avenues for improv-ing cross-Strait relations. This was a significant development in practical and symbolic terms, since it marked the end of the KMT and CCP's formal treatment of the other as mutual enemies. The two old rivals had yet again found a common purpose: opposition to Chen Shui-bian and the DPP's programme of Taiwanese nationalism.

The by-product of this new relationship was that the CCP and KMT became, in effect, business partners in the lucrative cross-Strait economy. When Ma succeeded Chen as president and the KMT won control of the Legislature in elections in 2008, numerous trade deals were quickly passed. But in Taiwan's situation, trade and investment with China is full of political significance and as Ma struck more and deeper deals with China, it produced a convulsive reaction from Taiwanese civil society. Concerned by the ramifications of Ma's policies for Taiwan's autonomy and capacity to resist unification, widespread protests and a student occupation of the Legislature became a watershed moment in Taiwanese politics known as the 2014 Sunflower Movement (see Chapter 3).

THE GEOPOLITICS OF SEMICONDUCTORS

When the sources of FDI that had helped ignite Taiwan's economic miracle began to slow in the 1970s and 1980s, the KMT regime responded with renewed domestic investment and major infrastructure projects to help spur domestic economic growth. The most consequential was state investment channelled into the technological industries. One of these industries was semiconductors. It was a farsighted decision, since semiconductors would become the backbone of the contemporary information age. They allow powerful and efficient flows of energy and electricity at a tiny scale, which is why they are used in almost every electronic device from consumer electronics, computers and automobiles to medical devices, military equipment and missiles. Without a regular supply of semiconductors the world as we know it would come to a standstill. Taiwan's capacity for manufacturing semiconductors is greater and more sophisticated than anywhere else in the world. Taiwan thus occupies a central place in global supply chains in many sectors and many categories of manufactured products.

In the late 1970s and 1980s information technology industries were changing the face of trade and economic growth in East Asian economies. Outside of Taiwan, South Korea and Japan were competing to attract international companies to produce technological components for computing equipment. While Taiwan was also part of this competition among its East Asian economic counterparts, it managed to create a unique competitive advantage for itself in the semiconductor industry. As Tsai and Cheng (2006: 5) describe, "If [Taiwan's] computer industry was built up by imitation, the semiconductor industry used innovation". The government and Taiwan's newly formed semiconductor companies invested heavily in R&D. They also actively recruited Taiwanese and Taiwanese American engineers to relocate to Hsinchu Science Park, established by the government in 1980 near Taipei. Many of these engineers were located in the US tech hub of Silicon Valley, the result of an earlier "brain drain" of Taiwanese talent. Networks between these Taiwanese and Taiwanese American engineers created enduring ties between Hsinchu and Silicon Valley and deepened US–Taiwan tech relations. The most important recruitment the Taiwanese government made was Morris Chang, the founder of Taiwan Semiconductor Manufacturing Corporation (TSMC), which would become one of the most important companies in the world.

No company defines semiconductor innovation better than TSMC. Established in 1987, TSMC redefined the importance of semiconductors and became the largest and most important semiconductor business in the world. TSMC supplies semiconductors to companies like Apple and Intel, and some estimates suggest that it controls half of the global market on made-to-order semiconductors, and 90 per cent of the market for advanced types of semiconductors. Headquartered in Hsinchu, TSMC is critical to the global economy. As industry expert Peter Hanbury put it, "They basically control the most complicated part of the semiconductor ecosystem, and they're a near monopoly at the bleeding edge" (Campbell 2021: n.p.).

TSMC's success story was unprecedented. Before its creation, Taiwan's role in the semiconductor supply chain was processing and packaging chips from Japan and for export around the world. Taiwan was set up for R&D on behalf of American and Japanese businesses rather than as an original manufacturer. But as Taiwanese engineers made sophisticated technological advances, it became clear that Taiwan could produce better semiconductors than Japanese, South Korean or American companies. The Taiwanese government recruited Chang from Texas Instruments to build Taiwan's semiconductor industry from the ground up. As Chris Miller describes in his book *Chip War*, the Taiwanese government offered Chang a blank cheque to build Taiwan's chip sector. Although Chang still had to secure private capital funding, TSMC "wasn't really a private business, it was a project of the Taiwanese state" (Miller 2022: 339).

Strong support from the Taiwanese government was not the only secret to TSMC's market success. What makes TSMC different from most other semiconductor companies is that they do not design chips, they only manufacture them. When Apple comes to TSMC, they have their own design for what kind of chips they want and TSMC provides their cutting-edge technological know-how to execute the design. By not designing their own chips and selling them to private firms, TSMC does not compete against its clients. Unlike Samsung, which designs and manufactures their own chips, TSMC is not loyal to any one company and can thus expand its partnerships in ways other private firms cannot.

TSMC's market share and technological edge remains second to none. Despite the aggressive efforts of its competitors, especially within China, to "catch up", every other semiconductor company in the world is years behind TSMC's current technological capabilities. TSMC's manufacturing facilities, engineers, and Taiwan-specific environment allows the company to both innovate and produce at a superior rate. Despite hundreds of imitators, no other semiconductor company has come close to reaching TSMC's capacities.

Increasing access and capacity in the semiconductor sector is a preoccupation for most of the world's advanced economies. In 2021, for instance, China reportedly spent more money importing semiconductors than oil (Sheng 2021). Access to Taiwanese chips is imperative for global economies – especially China and the US. The Covid-19 pandemic provided a taste of what losing access to Taiwanese semiconductors could mean for global production and supply chains across numerous sectors. It was during this global health crisis that many citizens around the world first realized how important semiconductors are to their everyday lives. Between the pandemic and deteriorating relations between the US and China, the role of TSMC and its Taiwanese counterparts was thrust into the global spotlight. Due to a combination of changing demand, supply-chain slow-down and the spread of Covid-19, the availability of chips for commodities like cars and computers was critically disrupted.

It suddenly became clear to consumers that semiconductors – and specifically Taiwan and TSMC – were an unseen but fundamental part of contemporary life (Lee 2021).

Global powers like the US and China do not only care about semiconductors for laptops and phones. Aside from consumer goods, many of the semiconductors used in US military technologies, from computers to missile systems, are made in Taiwan. Its own security threatened by the PRC, Taiwan is a key player in keeping some of the world's most sophisticated military technologies running. This fact partly explains why reliance on Taiwan for semiconductors has become a focal point for US government scrutiny. The CHIPS Act, a US policy passed in 2022 to boost investment and research in the domestic semiconductor sector, was in large part designed to reduce over-reliance on Taiwanese semiconductors. For now, the world's need for Taiwanese semiconductors – including many businesses in the PRC – continues to have significant geopolitical and geoeconomic implications.

In an op-ed for *Foreign Affairs* published in October 2021, President Tsai Ing-wen wrote that Taiwan's semiconductor industry acts as a "silicon shield" protecting Taiwan from "aggressive attempts by authoritarian regimes to disrupt global supply chains" (Tsai 2021). Tsai is not alone in seeing Taiwan's chip industry as a deterrent to PRC military action. Indeed, the idea of a "silicone shield" has currency among academics, policy analysts and industry experts. Related arguments have their merits and shortcomings.

The PRC would not benefit from a severe disruption to the global semiconductor supply chain. Losing TSMC, especially to a war, would be catastrophic for the world economy, including the PRC. Even in a hypothetical invasion scenario where TSMC survived unscathed, there is no guarantee that the PRC would be able to assume operations without the cooperation of TSMC's scientists and engineers. With TSMC investing around the world from Arizona to Germany, more companies are increasingly vested in the company – and Taiwan's – economic security. In a contemporary global economy where chips serve as a fundamental building block, Taiwan's semiconductor industry can be seen as a deterrent to war.

However, Taiwan's "silicone shield" is not a guarantee against conflict. There are multiple scenarios in which a major PLA military intervention, including invasion, could be "rational" even if it caused severe economic repercussions for the PRC. In the concluding chapter we set out numerous conflict scenarios. Under scenarios that threaten the authority or legitimacy of the CCP regime, or if the PRC's fundamental red lines are crossed, the cost–benefit calculus that has thus far prevented military conflict would likely change. Ultimately, the PRC's claim to sovereignty over Taiwan is not based on logics of global production, market competition or economic stability. When evaluating the merits of the "silicon shield" argument, it is important to keep in mind how nationalism and sovereignty can often trump economic security. Taiwan's semiconductor industry can deter conflict, and act as an incentive for all parties to manage contested preferences, but alone it cannot eradicate the potential for conflict.

TRADE POLICY TODAY

Despite stylized depictions of Taiwan's main parties' policy preferences, both the DPP and KMT favour continuing trade with China. What distinguishes their platforms is how trade is framed. The KMT argues that the Chinese market is crucial to Taiwan's economy. Furthermore, the KMT claims that its superior access and connections in the PRC allow the party to strike more advantageous economic deals for Taiwan. But if the Sunflower Movement taught us anything, it is that such trade deals do little to win over Taiwanese voters. The DPP frames trade with China rather differently. Although the DPP says that Taiwan ought to continue to trade with China, it is wary of Taiwan becoming over-reliant on the Chinese market, to the extent that it could be used as leverage by the PRC. Taiwan should therefore focus on diversifying its trade partners, expand its trade networks with other countries and regions and avoid overexposure to the PRC economy. A key example of the DPP's approach in practice is Tsai's signature New Southbound Policy, discussed in Chapter 9, which has focused on expanding economic ties between Taiwan and South and Southeast Asia.

Taiwan's lack of diplomatic recognition, combined with the PRC's strong opposition and influence, are formidable barriers to Taiwan's participation in formal bilateral or multilateral trade agreements.

Taiwan gained entry to the World Trade Organization (WTO), which does not require statehood for entry, shortly after the PRC in 2001. And while Taiwan is ever hopeful of joining multinational agreements like the Comprehensive and Progressive Agreement for Trans-Pacific Partnership (CPTPP), the big prize from an economic and political perspective would be a formal trade agreement with the United States. As president, Tsai Ing-wen pressed the US to enter into negotiations for some kind of bilateral trade agreement. To show Taiwan's commitment, she even went as far as to open Taiwan's markets to US pork, a long-term US requirement but a risky move in the context of Taiwanese domestic politics. Taiwanese public opinion has been strongly opposed to importing American meat because of the widespread use of ractopamine, a chemical added to animal feed that makes meat less fatty and leaner. The perception among Taiwanese publics, fanned by some politicians and media, is that ractopamine and similar chemical additives are harmful, despite peer-reviewed scientific research to the contrary.

When Tsai took the decision to open Taiwan's market to American pork it created a significant political backlash. Tsai's approval ratings were severely affected and the opposition KMT was able to mobilize support for a public referendum to be held on the question of US pork imports. In the referendum held in December 2021, Taiwanese voters rejected the KMT's proposal to reimpose a ban on American pork. This was a significant political victory for Tsai, and vindication of her bold gambit to kickstart trade talks. Amid the fallout from Pelosi's visit to Taiwan in August 2022, the US finally indicated its willingness to enter into preliminary negotiations. The first round of talks on the "US–Taiwan Initiative on 21st-Century Trade" took place in January 2023, organized by the institutions responsible for informal bilateral relations, namely the American Institute in Taiwan (AIT) and the Taipei Economic and Cultural Representative Office in the United States (TECRO).

DOMESTIC ECONOMIC CHALLENGES

Notwithstanding Taiwan's admirable record of stable growth, Taiwanese people face a number of challenges common to developed economies. Among these challenges are low wages and high housing costs. Taiwan has long been home to some of the slowest growing wages in the world. Its minimum wage is $5.62 an hour, which is 1.6 and 1.9 times lower than South Korea and Japan respectively. Housing in Taiwan meanwhile, is among the most expensive in the world. Per square metre, Taiwanese housing is more expensive than in both Japan and the United States (Ngerng 2022). Inequality is a significant issue in Taiwan, and especially apparent among young people unable to find jobs that pay highly enough to get on the housing ladder.

Why does Taiwan, given its experience of equitable economic development and continued growth, face these manifestations of inequality? Wealthy homeowners pay exceptionally low tax rates on their extra real estate or homes, creating low incentives to rent or sell at an affordable price. Taiwan's wealthy tend to hoard property and pay low wages to Taiwanese workers. These stubborn features of the Taiwanese economy have created conditions that keep middle-class growth slow and restrict upward mobility. Prices meanwhile have continued to rise, but wages have not matched the increase in the cost of living. Taiwan's minimum wage is rarely increased, and has spent the second longest duration without growth, behind only the US. As economic analyst Roy Ngerng notes, Taiwan's minimum wage is not adequate for the cost of living (Ngerng 2022). Wages have grown more under Tsai than under the previous two presidents, but still not enough to reverse growing inequality trends.

Even though many Taiwanese would like to elect politicians who promise higher wages and lower housing costs, few politicians ever make such policies part of their electoral platforms. Domestic economic problems rarely constitute voting issues. This is due to the salience of the China issue in Taiwanese electoral politics, but it is also the case that exploiting Taiwan's broken system of low wages and property hoarding is something that crosses party lines. Taiwanese business owners and landlords of all political persuasions take advantage of their economic position, regardless of domestic demand from middle and lower classes. Whether or not one supports independence, unification, or the status quo has little to do with recognizing that workers should be paid more. The fundamental challenge for labour and housing activists is convincing Taiwanese politicians and voters to take these issues seriously while not detracting from priority issues like cross-Strait relations.

Even though Taiwan was able to boast strong economic growth throughout the pandemic, it is important to keep in mind the disparity of this growth. With enterprises like the semiconductor industry accounting for so much of Taiwan's export sector, the big numbers reflected in overall GDP are not making their way down to middle- and working-class Taiwanese. Instead, most people in Taiwanese society have seen minimal increases in income, but face higher costs of living as a result of Covid-19.

Taiwan's economic transformation, the scope of its international trade and its world-leading semiconductor industry have fostered intense regional and global interactions. In the next chapter, we expand the definition of international participation from purely economic interactions to those that occur in the contested domain related to Taiwan's status.

9

Taiwan's international position

It is an accepted heuristic to describe Taiwan as marginalized. That description is not entirely accurate, since it conflates several aspects of international interactions. Taiwan is marginalized in the sense that it has a mere 13 formal diplomatic allies and is barred from participation in many international organizations as a result of PRC opposition. This situation continues despite growing international support for Taiwan's participation in organizations that affect the material well-being of Taiwan's 24 million people, such as the World Health Organization (WHO), or the safety of Taiwanese and others, such as the International Civil Aviation Organization (ICAO). Since both of these examples are specialized organizations under the United Nations, the PRC's veto power means Taiwan's participation is entirely by the PRC's grace.

During the period of Ma's China-friendly policies, the PRC allowed Taiwan to participate as an observer, only to retract this favour when Tsai Ing-wen won the presidency. There are other organizations that Taiwan can participate in where statehood is not a precondition for membership. But participation is still usually contingent on doing so under a name that meets the PRC's demand that it does not hint at recognition of Taiwanese sovereignty. Taiwanese representative teams can only compete at the Olympics and other international sporting competitions under the otherwise meaningless name of "Chinese Taipei" (there is no such place or entity). Taiwan participates in the WTO as the Separate Customs Territory of Taiwan, Penghu, Kinmen and Matsu, and appears in WTO communications as Chinese Taipei. Taiwan is represented in some other organizations, but the indignities it suffers to do so are incongruous given its standing as a major global economy, technology powerhouse and successful liberal democracy. It is a loss to the international community, as demonstrated during the Covid-19 pandemic when Taiwan was excluded from receiving guidance from the WHO – and from contributing its expertise. For Taiwanese people it is also a matter of national dignity and pride. However, this does not mean that Taiwan should only be seen as marginalized.

TAIWANESE OVERSEAS

In terms of informal diplomatic relations, trade, civil society connections and people-to-people exchanges facilitated by previous waves of migration and the great mobility of Taiwanese people today, Taiwan engages intensely with the outside world. In addition to the high level of economic trade discussed in Chapter 8, Taiwan also sends significant numbers of students, skilled workers and tourists overseas. Taiwan itself is highly international, with an increasing diversity of peoples and cultures visible in major cities. The Taiwanese diaspora is considerable, with concentrations in the US, Japan and Southeast Asia. Additionally, there are social organizations, friendship associations and NGOs promoting Taiwan and Taiwanese causes. They can be influential in lobbying support for Taiwan, such as the US-based Formosan Association for Public Affairs (FAPA), a non-profit with chapters around the world promoting Taiwan independence.

One other group of Taiwanese expats is large and significant, namely the communities of professionals and businesspeople (*Taishang*) based in the PRC. Attracted by economic opportunities as the PRC opened up to Taiwanese investment, and encouraged by cultural and linguistic affinities, proximity (especially after direct flight routes were authorized), or family ties, large communities of *Taishang* began emerging in the PRC in the 2000s. At one point in the mid-2010s this community of entrepreneurs, businesspeople and multinational workers was said to number around one million people, with a particular concentration around Shanghai. Often living semi-permanently in the PRC, they would return to Taiwan periodically to see family, receive subsidized medical care, or to vote in elections. The phenomenon became a political issue, with scepticism about the loyalties of Taiwanese citizens who choose to live in the PRC. Perhaps, the concern went, their voting decisions would not reflect the interests of Taiwanese who lived in Taiwan all the time. Despite such suspicions, this cohort did not become a "fifth column" and since reaching a high point during Ma Ying-jeou's presidency, the number of *Taishang* has declined significantly. Without Taiwanese consular or legal representation, and facing an increasingly difficult business environment and dwindling comparative advantages, *Taishang* have returned in substantial numbers to Taiwan, or moved to developing world locations where the regulatory environment, costs and work conditions are more favourable.

Concerns about *Taishang* as a social class exerting undue influence in Taiwanese politics have largely proven unfounded. However, that is not to say that individuals with business interests and intensive interactions with the PRC have not created issues in Taiwanese society. Several Taiwanese entrepreneurs have used their economic power to promote unification or policies that would facilitate Chinese influence over Taiwanese society. One high profile example is Tsai Eng-meng, a Taiwanese entrepreneur who made his fortune selling instant noodles and building a snack food empire in the PRC. Tsai is a vocal proponent of unification, and has put his wealth behind it by investing in major media operations in Taiwan. His Want Want Media Group has acquired various media platforms and altered editorial lines to suit a more China-friendly position. Tsai's accumulation of television channels, newspapers and media groups led to widespread public concerns about the concentration of media ownership in the hands of an owner whose business interests were so exposed to the PRC market and whose control over the venerable *China Times* newspaper had already seen it become a purveyor of China-friendly positions. Coinciding with Ma's accelerated detente policies, public angst triggered a student-led protest movement, the Anti-Media Monopoly Movement in 2012, which ultimately led to legislation (the Anti-Media Monopoly Act) to prevent the distortion of Taiwan's information environment (Rawnsley & Feng 2014).

TAIWAN AS REGIONAL AND GLOBAL DEMOCRACY

Throughout her tenure as president, Tsai Ing-wen worked assiduously to position Taiwan as a member of the global community of liberal democracies. The rationale for this discursive and policy strategy is obvious: Taiwan is a democracy that is facing an existential threat, in terms of the exercise of ROC sovereignty and the continuation of its democratic system, from an authoritarian neighbour. Taiwan's most consequential supporter, to the extent that it acts as de facto security guarantor, is also a democracy and is engaged in strategic rivalry with the PRC (i.e. the US). And as many other democracies reconsider their relations with China and react to the PRC's domestic and international actions and ambitions it has become clear that there are shared interests with Taiwan.

The calculation within the Tsai administration was that international support for Taiwan among democratic nations, which largely constitute the West, could act as a deterrent to PRC military action. The unified western response to Russia's invasion of Ukraine, including sanctions and supply of weapons, concretized that notion. The PRC is vastly more powerful than Russia, its economy is more diversified, self-sufficient and globalized, but increasingly vocal and tangible international support for Taiwan is a complicating factor in the PRC's decision-making. The internationalization of the Taiwan issue is welcomed by Taiwan and the US, and anathema to the PRC, which frequently reiterates that it is an "internal Chinese matter" and that it will not accept "external interference". Any suggestion of external interference, substantive or ideational, prompts the PRC to react, and this potential has for many years circumscribed commercial and diplomatic actors' willingness to engage with Taiwan.

However, there are signs of change, as the West reconsiders its relationship with the PRC. President Tsai actively and cannily sought to leverage this change. In Tsai's discourse the juxtaposition of Taiwan and the PRC in terms of democratic values recurred frequently. In a bifurcating world she situated Taiwan firmly in the community of global democracies, and on the frontline standing up against the expansion of authoritarianism. She positioned Taiwan as a responsible stakeholder, upholder of the international rules-based order and a contributor of public goods. The internationalization of the Taiwan Strait is in Taiwan's strategic interest, as other countries signal their opposition to PRC coercion and unilateral efforts to change the status quo.

Taiwan cannot change its fundamental geography, but Tsai sought to reimagine Taiwan as a regional and international actor. For example, her New Southbound Policy positioned Taiwan not just as a cross-Strait economy, but one literally and metaphorically invested in the broader Asian region. In Tsai's discourse, Taiwan was framed as an Indo-Pacific economy and a democracy in the global contest over liberal values. Through these discursive constructions, Tsai tried to establish that cross-Strait relations were not merely the business of Taiwan and China, but of regional and global concern. While this construction appeared to resonate in many western countries, practical efforts to build on the rhetoric are irreconcilable with PRC opposition to Taiwan's continued autonomy, international participation, and sensitivity to "external interference". Tsai argued that irrespective of PRC opposition, Taiwan must continue to establish and expand international connections, while advocating a low-key approach to building unofficial, informal relationships to avoid, as much as possible, provoking PRC sensitivities.

TAIWAN'S MODES OF DIPLOMACY

Taiwan's public diplomacy has come a long way in recent years (Newland 2022). Although many Taiwanese politicians were early adopters of new forms of communication domestically and especially as part of their election campaigning repertoire, external communications took a long time to catch up. The institution in charge of communicating Taiwan to the outside world, the Government Information Office (GIO), was cumbersome, slow and opaque. It was often difficult, as an outsider, to get information on Taiwan. The GIO's main outputs consisted of propaganda-style pamphlets or unappealing brochures in small print. Taiwanese politicians, satisfied with communicating solely with domestic audiences, for a long time resisted global digital and social media platforms. In that regard the Tsai administration has been transformative. Tsai herself was active on all major platforms, notably Twitter, where she has a substantial international following. Her foreign minister, Joseph Wu, was an active commentator on international affairs as they pertain to Taiwan. The government system for international communications now responds quickly, lines of command and decision-making systems having been radically streamlined. Teams attached to the government have been professionalized and produce content that is timely and impactful.

The Covid-19 pandemic provides a good illustration of Taiwanese-style public diplomacy (Yen 2020). Once Taiwan's own gold-standard pandemic response was initiated, government accounts launched an international social media campaign around the hashtag #TaiwanCanHelp. The message was that Taiwan stood ready to provide personal protective equipment, medical equipment and expertise to countries suffering from Covid waves. Government officials and civil society actors coalesced around the campaign, with generous offers to share Taiwan's experience, expertise and surplus medical equipment and supplies. While the sentiment was surely altruistic and genuine, the message was also a strategic fit for the image Taiwan wants to present as a responsible stakeholder willing to provide the region and the world with public goods. The evolution of the campaign is also illustrative. Blocked from participation in the WHO at the height of a once-in-a-century global pandemic, and with potential recipients of Taiwanese help discouraged by the PRC, the hashtag changed from #TaiwanCanHelp to the plaintive #LetTaiwanHelp.

Tsai Ing-wen described her mode of diplomacy as "steadfast", with an emphasis on maintaining formal and informal support for Taiwan in the international realm based on mutuality and reciprocal benefits. Despite adopting a cautious position on cross-Strait relations that emphasized "maintaining the status quo", the PRC froze diplomatic contact from the start of Tsai's presidency, cutting direct communications, resuming its block on Taiwan's international participation, and inducing ROC diplomatic allies to switch sides. Why would the PRC cut ties with an apparent moderate and pragmatist on cross-Strait policy?

From the PRC's perspective, it does not matter how reasonable a politician Tsai actually was, since her refusal to acknowledge One China and accept the 1992 Consensus were immediate dealbreakers. However, the CCP's undifferentiated approach to DPP politicians is a problem. Casting the DPP as a "separatist" party that must not be engaged blocks dialogue between Taiwan and the PRC for years at a time – for the 16-year duration of Chen Shui-bian and Tsai Ing-wen's tenures. Conceptually flattening all DPP politicians is a missed opportunity to engage in dialogue with DPP moderates like Tsai. But, to the CCP, Tsai is no different from a radical advocate of Taiwan independence, when her pragmatism may actually have presented an opportunity for dialogue.

Over the course of the Tsai administrations, the PRC eroded Taiwan's already minimal formal diplomatic recognition to just 12 states plus the Vatican. Despite these losses, which are more psychologically harmful than likely to erode the ROC's foundations for functional autonomy, Tsai determined that Taiwan would not compete with the PRC to curry favour with allies tempted to switch allegiances. She argued that an earlier Taiwanese policy known colloquially as "dollar diplomacy" had had a destabilizing effect on numerous small developing nations, where political factions would compete on the basis of whether they promoted relations with the ROC or PRC (Rich & Dahmer 2022). In some countries, like the Solomon Islands, competition between factions on the basis of "which China?" led to instability, corruption and violence. Refusing to engage in such distorting and destabilizing practices fit Tsai's efforts to frame Taiwan as a responsible global stakeholder.

Spending on diplomatic recognition efforts that led to excessive aid demands from allies that saw ties with Taiwan in instrumental terms was also unpopular with Taiwanese taxpayers (Rich & Dahmer 2020). But it does not mean that Taiwan has stopped spending to maintain its small number of remaining allies, or lavishing leaders of allies with state visits and generous investment deals. It is possible that the PRC, if it decided to do so, could induce most or all of the ROC's remaining allies to switch. With the exception of the Vatican, Taiwan's allies are small and economically needy. However, the PRC has shown that its strategy is to pick them off piecemeal. The utility of this strategy is twofold. It provides a handy signalling device when the PRC is displeased with something Taiwan has done. And it can be used at challenging moments in Taiwanese domestic politics in order to inflict maximum damage on the Taiwanese government *du jour*. The only globally significant ally of the ROC is the Vatican. The PRC, however, has invested significant diplomatic efforts trying to woo the Holy See, and concessions agreed by the Catholic Patriotic Association (i.e. the Chinese Catholic church) in 2018 over the issue of episcopal appointments hinted at improved prospects.

TAIWANESE SOFT POWER

As a liberal democracy with an active civil society, world-class capacities in technology, medicine and science, and a hybrid culture that is increasingly celebrated for its diversity, Taiwan is well-placed with regard to soft power reserves. The exercise of Taiwanese soft power is subject to some circumscriptions as a result of PRC opposition to Taiwan's international participation. However, there are many areas in which Taiwan has exercised its advantages in this sphere. Taiwan's cultural and creative industries have produced internationally acclaimed film, music and dance. The entertainment and popular cultural sectors have seen Taiwanese pop music, television dramas and celebrities gain traction across Asia. Many Taiwanese celebrities have been very successful in the PRC market. In some cases they have had to modify their statements relating to One China or reject support for the DPP, but those willing to self-censor or genuinely hold beliefs that are consistent with PRC policy have been embraced by Chinese audiences.

As working conditions in the PRC have become more difficult with the tightening of all social sectors under Xi Jinping, Taiwan has welcomed multinational firms, expatriate workers and foreign journalists to set up their operations in Taipei (Olcott 2022). Although Taiwan was able to benefit from such relocations, cumbersome bureaucracy, low wages, and a tight labour market led some of these new firms and investors to leave Taiwan prematurely (Cheng 2022). Despite Taiwan's need for bureaucratic reform, the juxtaposition of Taiwan's organic, civil society-led soft power activities and the PRC's less nimble state-authored initiatives has enhanced international perceptions of Taiwan. Much to the chagrin of the PRC, which sees its own development achievements subsumed by a predominantly negative and critical western focus on its political system, human rights and foreign policy.

TSAI ING-WEN'S ECONOMIC DIPLOMACY

As an advisor to Lee Teng-hui, Tsai was one of the architects of the original Go South policy in the mid-1990s. As ROC president, her New Southbound Policy (NSP) was significantly more ambitious, multidimensional and long term. The NSP sets out a vision for regional cooperation that goes beyond the instrumentality and short-termism that ultimately doomed previous versions of the policy. The NSP also goes beyond trade and economic linkages to foreground people-to-people exchanges and resource sharing across the medical, education, agricultural and tech sectors. There is an emphasis on investment in capital and technology-intensive sectors, and a move away from unilateral outward Taiwanese investment to embrace southbound capital – and migrants – to Taiwan.

The geographical scope of the NSP now covers the ten ASEAN countries, six South Asian nations, and Australia and New Zealand. Ultimately, the NSP is geared to leveraging Taiwan's prowess in science, technology and medicine, promoting both functional cooperation, expanding Taiwanese "soft power" and establishing Taiwan as a more integral actor in the Indo-Pacific region. Tsai's discourse framed Taiwan as a responsible regional stakeholder, able and willing to contribute public goods to regional development. Tsai was also at pains to avoid the impression that the NSP was in competition with the Belt and Road Initiative, the PRC's global scale infrastructure project that became their vision of Chinese-led globalization. The NSP cannot compete with the Belt and Road Initiative in terms of funding or ambition, but that is not the point. It seeks to provide support for Taiwanese firms to invest and develop business away from the PRC market, and to leverage complementarities with other economies. Taiwan is a member of the WTO, acceding shortly after the PRC in 2001, but its participation in regional free trade agreements, like CPTPP, is complicated by PRC opposition. The NSP is therefore a useful policy tool for expanding Taiwan's regional embeddedness and diversifying away from the PRC. To date, the NSP has avoided politicization and the PRC has not pressured constituent countries to disengage, possibly because China's own intense economic engagement and diplomatic leverage in Southeast Asia gives it the confidence to downplay the NSP's significance.

10

Taiwan's future

Taiwan is a dynamic polity and cross-Strait relations are volatile. And broader US–China relations are in flux, if not at an inflection point. The dynamic changes in politics and foreign relations that we have discussed in the preceding chapters are an indication that nothing can be taken for granted. It is therefore difficult to predict Taiwan's future. Nonetheless, having evaluated some of the major issues surrounding Taiwan, we conclude by looking to the future and highlighting key questions and uncertainties.

THE POST-TSAI ERA

Tsai Ing-wen's two-term presidency concludes in 2024 with great uncertainty about her possible successor and the direction Taiwanese politics and cross-Strait relations takes next. Reflecting on the Tsai era, we see a consequential leader who made a significant imprint on Taiwan's trajectory. Domestically, she made a number of difficult policy reforms that were not universally well received. A volatile first term saw the passage of necessary labour and pension reforms that damaged her approval ratings. At one point it was not even certain that she would stand for re-election. Her second term was largely defined by Covid-19 and national security. Taiwan's pandemic policy response was globally lauded and led to some of the best Covid-19 outcomes in the world. Tsai's effective leadership led to strong approval ratings until subsequent economic slowdown began to be felt in Taiwan.

The verdict on Tsai coming out of western capitals was more unanimously positive. Tsai was praised for her pragmatism and moderation, her caution with regard to Chinese red lines and her preference for substance over symbolism. The same moderation toward China was criticized by some of the DPP's more radical supporters. KMT supporters meanwhile decried the same policies as futile and needlessly antagonistic toward the PRC, jeopardizing Taiwan's security and economy. Despite these dual critiques, Tsai persevered and was rewarded with a high level of trust in the western international community. The scale of Tsai's feat in securing Washington DC's approval, and rehabilitating the DPP's reputation after the Chen Shui-bian era, should not be underestimated. Furthermore, she set a high new standard for Taiwan's leadership internationally.

Where does Taiwan go after Tsai? Regardless of the next president's political affiliation, they will inherit a full slate of serious issues. Internationally, they need to assure crucial allies like the US that Taiwan will continue to adhere to Tsai's pragmatism. How China receives the incoming president will determine how cross-Strait relations develop during a crucial period when the military balance equalizes. While the KMT can promise more cooperative relations with China, it must balance Taiwan's close relationship with the US. The DPP, which has no lines of communication to the Chinese leadership, must adopt policies that continue to balance keeping Taiwan free without risking its security.

One of the most important policy continuities is the future of military reforms in Taiwan. Tsai prioritized strengthening ROC forces, including taking on unpopular reforms to military conscription, increasing national service obligations from four months to one year. The scope of PLA live-fire drills in August 2022 highlighted the advances that the PRC has made in its operational capabilities, and increased the urgency of Taiwan's defensive preparations. The extent to which further needed military reforms and budget requests will be addressed by the new administration and passed by the new Legislature is uncertain. Taiwan needs better invasion and blockade preparedness, while boosting civil society's faith and trust in the government and military. Continuing to cultivate resolve in civil society remains a significant responsibility for the next president.

XI JINPING'S THIRD TERM

In October 2022 Xi Jinping was re-elected general secretary of the CCP and chair of the Central Military Commission by delegates to the 20th National Congress of the Chinese Communist Party (NPC). In other words, Xi's leadership of the party and the PLA were confirmed for another five-year term. A further five-year term as president of China was conferred separately in March 2023. Xi placed allies in positions of power throughout the Standing Committee, the seven-person pinnacle of Chinese power, and the broader Politburo. Xi's dominance was embodied in amendments to the party constitution, which consolidated the "core status" of Xi and Xi Thought at the heart of the CCP. No successor was anointed, and it is possible that Xi will continue to rule China for another decade.

Xi has personally directed the robust transformation of China's foreign posture toward the US and toward Taiwan. Furthermore, he has invested considerable political capital in the project to "rejuvenate the great Chinese nation" from which "complete unification of the motherland" is indivisible. Xi has spoken of this "sacred task" and does not conceal the urgency with which he wants to achieve unification. Further amendments to the party constitution reiterated the use of force to prevent "Taiwan independence" and the goal of unification under the auspices of "one country, two systems". Speculation that Xi has enlisted Wang Huning, a trusted lieutenant and the brains behind many of Xi's political programmes, to come up with new thinking on Taiwan remains to be seen.

Xi Jinping and the PLA's game plan for Taiwan is uncertain. Reports about the possibility of military action in 2027, the year in which the US expects the military balance to tilt and which also marks the centenary of the PLA's founding, are speculative. No one really knows if Xi has a grand strategy for Taiwan or what kind of contingencies the PLA is planning for. And despite current trajectories, there is still room for both cross-Strait and US–China relations to return to the former equilibrium. It is important to consider that the capacity and the intention to employ military force are separate issues. The PLA's capabilities and the PRC's threats towards Taiwan have increased under Xi, but there is no hard evidence that military action, much less a full-scale invasion, is on the horizon. In his rhetoric, Xi has implied that he does not intend to leave unification to his successors. Yet, the decision to go to war would incur a high risk for the PRC and the CCP. What level of risk the CCP would consider tolerable is uncertain, as is the leadership's information and calculus.

THE FUTURE OF CROSS-STRAIT RELATIONS

The position of Taiwan's major political parties and western countries' One China policies is that Taiwanese people should have a say in any resolution of the Taiwan issue. In practice, although not imminent, that implies that moves toward unification would require Taiwanese people to vote in favour of it. Public opinion does not suggest that is likely (Rigger *et al.* 2021), neither the longitudinal polls on national identity and national status discussed in Chapter 3, nor recent data on attitudes toward the PRC. Taiwanese have increasingly negative perceptions of the PRC and "one country, two systems" has negligible appeal. In 2021, one survey showed 90 per cent of Taiwanese rejected the prospect of "one country, two systems" (CNA 2021). The ongoing curtailing of liberties in China, the crackdown in Hong Kong and the threatening posture toward Taiwan have, unsurprisingly, failed to win Taiwanese hearts and minds.

Is there another solution that could be attractive to Taiwanese people? The "one country, two systems" proposal for Taiwan was first conceived many decades ago, and although Taiwanese elites and publics have never shown much interest, the PRC has not deviated from it. This suggests that it is as generous an offer as the PRC can envisage for a peaceful unification solution. The CCP's position on Taiwan, relentlessly repeated in the Chinese information environment, has created pressures that preclude greater compromise. The insistence that the DPP is not to be negotiated with until it accepts One China has eliminated room for manoeuvre, even under a pragmatist like Tsai. The CCP is willing to work with the KMT, but there is no suggestion that the KMT's preferences or capacity to turn Taiwanese public opinion might yield unification either. A staccato cycle in cross-Strait relations has thus taken hold: cooperation but little prospect of unification with KMT governments, frozen and conflictual relations under DPP governments.

US POLICY TOWARD TAIWAN

US–Taiwan relations have seldom been in a healthier state. To put it in President Biden's often-repeated phrase, American support for Taiwan is "rock solid". It should not escape attention that US–China and US–Taiwan relations have been tracking an inverse trajectory. Indeed a negative correlation between the health of US–Taiwan and US–China relations is observable historically. For better and for worse, Taiwan's prosperity and security is implicated in the relationship between these two superpowers, which it is compelled to navigate as best it can. Increasing rivalry between the US and China has benefitted Taiwan in terms of securing greater American support. Yet, there is a current in Taiwanese public opinion that is critical of Taiwan's reliance on the US. Some arguments decry the patronage of either superpower, while others point out that Taiwan is vulnerable to the vicissitudes of an external relationship in which it has no agency. For now, the many manifestations of US–China strategic rivalry look set to keep the US engaged on Taiwan, but a significant change in US foreign policy priorities or in US–China relations could seriously affect Taiwan's security.

Although US support, from provision of weapons to a potential bilateral trade deal, is generally received with gratitude in Taiwan, it does not come without costs and risk. As the fallout from Speaker Pelosi's visit showed, it is inevitably Taiwan rather than the US that faces the repercussions. The increasing salience of China as a political issue in the US and the rise of bipartisan hawkishness, has in some cases been channelled into ostensibly "supportive" statements or gestures toward Taiwan. The benefit that Taiwan accrues from such symbolic and rhetorical actions is less certain. Some American political rhetoric is also not well considered. The comments made by Mike Pompeo cited in Chapter 6 is one of numerous examples. Of the American politicians inspired to speak in similarly unguarded ways about Taiwan, how many are motivated by animosity towards the PRC or domestic rewards for their posturing rather than a desire to support outcomes for Taiwan that Taiwanese themselves support? Notwithstanding this scepticism, there is clearly genuine appreciation for Taiwan in the US political firmament, and it has meaningful implications for Taiwan and the broader Indo-Pacific region.

The campaign and vote in the US presidential election in November 2024 will be closely watched in Taiwan. China is likely to feature prominently, and electoral candidates may be incentivized to adopt hostile positions toward China and concomitant supportive positions toward Taiwan. Our hope is that US politicians consider what form of support is most appropriate for Taiwan. From a Taiwanese perspective, refusing American support, even when it arrives in a form that complicates Taiwan's situation, is unrealistic. Instead of assuming what Taiwan wants, American politicians and officials should ask what Taiwanese people need from US support. To that end, Congressional delegations, unofficial institutions and close communications between the two sides are welcome. US policy is naturally self-interested, but there is a high degree of overlap between American and Taiwanese preferences: neither side wants war with China, neither side wants a PRC-controlled Taiwan, and to the greatest extent possible, both sides want productive relations with each other and with China.

REGIONAL GEOPOLITICS

Taiwan and Ukraine are not analogous situations, but there are significant resonances. The CCP leadership has watched the world's reaction to the Russian invasion closely. One of the most important takeaways for Taiwan is how the western world has united against Russia and provided support to Ukraine. The unity and depth of international sanctions and supply of weapons likely took Vladimir Putin and Xi Jinping by surprise. This does not mean the same level of support is guaranteed to Taiwan, or the same punitive measures levelled against the PRC in the event of PLA military action. It is, however, an input for Xi's strategic calculus. How the world reacts to the end of the war in Ukraine will also heavily influence Taiwan. The endgame and outcome of the war are uncertain, with China itself attempting to play a diplomatic role. How Russia and Ukraine emerge from the war will be watched closely in China to see whether the sanctions regime continues or Russia is rehabilitated and the extent to which Ukraine is integrated into the western security and political orders. Taiwan is learning from Ukraine too, for example in protecting critical infrastructure, cultivating international support and preparing its civilian population for resistance.

The status quo in East Asian security is less robust than in the past few decades. This is in large part a function of the actions and perceived intentions of China and the US, and the geopolitics of an increasingly competitive relationship. Countries in the region have responded to these dynamics, and evidently perceive Taiwan, in addition to the broader South China Sea, as a focal point of Asian (in)security. Regional actors like Japan, South Korea, the Philippines and others have responded to instability and threats to peace in the Taiwan Strait. Notably, Japan has already begun to bolster its military capacity in preparation for a potential military conflict close to its borders. Japan and Taiwan have a strong unofficial relationship and even though Japan is not yet fully committed to assisting Taiwan in the event of an attack from the PRC, the likelihood of its intervention is high (Liff 2022). South Korea has made fewer commitments than Japan, but a conflict so close to its borders would also require a response from Seoul. The Philippines, the Southeast Asian country closest to Taiwan, has already begun establishing a refugee policy for Taiwanese in the event of a military crisis (RTI 2022). A military conflict over Taiwan would have far-reaching ramifications on regional security, economy and diplomacy, and it is important to observe the preparations and policies of regional actors. However, conflict in the Taiwan Strait is a geopolitical issue and preparations are not localized to Northeast Asia. Every country in the Indo-Pacific is thinking through their course of action and contingency planning in the event of a war over Taiwan. So are European actors like France and the UK, which recognize that Indo-Pacific security is a global issue.

WHAT MIGHT CAUSE WAR IN THE TAIWAN STRAIT?

The PRC position since 1979 has been to pursue "peaceful unification" while retaining and refining its military options in order to prevent "Taiwan independence". The risks for the CCP involved in a decision to launch a significant military action against Taiwan are very consequential. An invasion attempt, in particular, is only conceivable in a scenario where either the CCP regime faces collapse (for example as the result of internal social collapse) or the calculus is that Taiwan would otherwise be "lost". One scenario where the latter is imaginable involves

Taiwan signalling an imminent declaration of independence. If the US or other western powers were to show support for such a move, the PRC's calculation would be even more straightforward. However, such a scenario is currently unthinkable. There is no indication that a declaration of independence is a political possibility in Taiwan, nor that any other nations would support it. Short of this extreme hypothetical situation, there are other scenarios that might precipitate a PLA military action against Taiwan.

First, the US recognizes the ROC. If the US conferred formal diplomatic recognition on the ROC, the PRC would certainly interpret it as being equivalent to American recognition of "Taiwan independence". This scenario would necessitate a military response from the PRC to prevent the formalization of "Two Chinas". Despite the US probing the edges of its One China policy, it is currently inconceivable that the US would pursue this course of action given the inevitable response from the PRC.

Second, a dramatic change in the US or PRC military situation. The military situation in the Taiwan Strait has been relatively stable for decades. Despite the PLA's modernization, an equilibrium with an acceptable level of background threat was arrived at. However, the calculus would change if the US hypothetically sought to sell or install offensive weapons on Taiwan. Similarly, if the US were to propose stationing troops or naval ships in Taiwanese ports. The dangers involved in such a move are well known and unlikely. A different change in the military situation would be if the PLA revealed an unforeseen tilt in the military balance such that PRC forces significantly outweigh those of Taiwan and the US. The PLA's preparations for kinetic action in the Taiwan Strait theatre have eroded the advantages that Taiwan and the US once enjoyed, however a full attack would require an unimaginably large gap in capacities in order to render it low risk. It is unlikely that the PLA would be able to establish such an advantage in the near or mid term.

Third, PLA overconfidence and miscalculation. None of these scenarios appears as likely as a risky action prompted by overconfidence in the PLA's capacity and an underestimation of the capacity and resolve of Taiwan and the US. It is possible to imagine this kind of decision being influenced by insufficient or erroneous intelligence reports, pressure to act emanating from hawkish officials in the PLA and CCP or from an uncontrolled groundswell of nationalist sentiment triggered by actions by Taiwan or the US. Xi Jinping's concentration of power and appointment of loyalists to positions of power in the Select Committee and Politburo potentially compromise objective intelligence and strategic assessments. The potential for PLA hubris or for the CCP to be swayed by the hardline preferences of popular nationalism is cited by arguments in favour of more explicit US signalling and strategic clarity. To date, the PRC has generally exercised restraint in its actions toward Taiwan, despite periodic military demonstrations in the Strait.

Fourth, CCP regime endangered by domestic strife. The level of risk involved in full-scale military action against Taiwan is so high that for the CCP to make this decision would be an act of desperation, either because it fears "losing" Taiwan or because the regime itself faces a severe or existential threat. In a desperation scenario the CCP's strategic calculus would be more risk acceptant, increasing the likelihood of action against Taiwan. The PRC faces many economic and social issues, and in the absence of democratic mechanisms the continuation of the regime requires the consent of the Chinese population. A combination of societal controls, mastery of the domestic information environment and genuine sources of performance legitimacy has secured this consent, and a protracted economic downturn or protest movement of sufficient severity to erode the regime's legitimacy is unforeseeable.

Fifth, crisis of CCP legitimacy or authority. Taiwan has become such an impassioned issue in contemporary PRC nationalism that it has the potential to be invoked in response to crises of legitimacy or authority. Unification by force as a means to restoring lost legitimacy could be an option for the CCP. Alternatively, if Xi Jinping were to feel his authority under threat, attacking Taiwan to re-establish control is an imaginable scenario. Currently, there is no sign that either the CCP or Xi's authority are under threat.

Sixth, societal disintegration in Taiwan. If Taiwanese society encountered some kind of catastrophic social chaos or disintegration, the PRC has stated on numerous occasions that it might necessitate military intervention to uphold the integrity of the Chinese nation and to prevent Taiwan coming under the control of an outside enemy. Since Taiwan's political, economic and social situations are stable and highly functional, there is no indication that such a development is likely.

Finally, Taiwan's indefinite rejection of unification. Less dramatic and more incremental than those scenarios listed above, it involves Taiwan demonstrating, perhaps through legislation or constitutional amendments, that it permanently rejects the possibility of unification. This is not the same thing as declaring "independence", indeed it would imply a rejection of "Taiwan independence" in favour of the preservation of the ROC. Compared to the previous scenarios, this one is more plausible. Over several decades military force was conceived as a deterrent to "Taiwan independence". But a new PRC understanding of "independence" as Taiwan's prolonged separation under its existing de facto autonomy, combined with a refusal to indicate openness or progress towards unification, might be considered grounds for military action. This scenario is concerning since the PRC has not explicitly indicated what kind of Taiwanese action, or non-action, would lead to this assessment.

FINAL THOUGHTS

When we began writing this book in August 2022 Taiwan was a mainstay of the 24-hour news cycle in the US and Europe. It quickly became obvious to us that the scope and depth of coverage did not match the quantity of Taiwan's mentions on news channel chyrons. We decided then to write something that went beyond the headlines, but was still accessible to readers coming to Taiwan for the first time or without much prior exposure. We have argued for Taiwan to be taken seriously on its own merits and hope that this book will stimulate interest in learning more. Taiwan is one of the freest societies in East Asia, and indicators like press freedom, quality of life, and social equality suggest it will continue to develop in that direction. Fellow democracies around the world show increasing interest in supporting Taiwan to preserve its autonomy and resist a less free future authored by the PRC. Concerned citizens around the world rightly worry about Taiwan's future.

Taiwan's status however, is precarious. With its intractable claim to sovereignty and its leaders' increasing frustration with Taiwan's de facto independence, the PRC represents a credible threat to Taiwanese security. Currently, every indication shows that Taiwanese people do not favour unification. This act of resistance, in the face of serious external threat, has attracted an unprecedented amount of international attention in the past year. Our hope is that this interest will be directed to listening to Taiwanese voices and to Taiwan on its own merits. Superpower politics and the conflict are the dominant lenses through which Taiwan is seen internationally, but Taiwanese agency and the complexity and diversity of Taiwanese wants and needs deserve to be heard.

Glossary

1992 Consensus A meeting that took place between representatives from the PRC and ROC in 1992 under which a supposed "consensus" over each sides attitudes towards defining Taiwan's position to China.

Benshengren Han Chinese who lived in Taiwan prior to the KMT's arrival.

CCP Chinese Communist Party (also rendered CPC, Communist Party of China).

Chinese Taipei The name adopted by Taiwan in order to participate in international events such as the Olympics

DPP Democratic Progressive Party, the political party founded during Taiwan's democratization which advocates for Taiwanese sovereignty.

KMT The Chinese Nationalist Party, the political party originally from China that fled to Taiwan who advocate for closer relations with China.

NPP The New Power Party, founded by activists after the 2014 Sunflower Movement, this party is explicitly pro-independence, and in the past has allied with the DPP, but currently is more critical of the ruling party.

One-China policy The United States' policy that states it acknowledges the PRC's claims to Taiwan, but does not recognize them.

One-China principle The PRC's policy that there is only one China, governed by the PRC, and Taiwan is part of China.

one country, two systems A formulation first promoted by the PRC for administering a post-unification Taiwan and subsequently adopted in post-handover Hong Kong. It provides a theoretical and legal basis for political and governance systems in Chinese sovereign territories distinct from those on the Chinese mainland. In theory, this includes a "high degree of autonomy", political representation and other features not present in mainland China itself.

PLA People's Liberation Army.

PRC People's Republic of China, the regime founded by Mao Zedong in 1949 after defeating the KMT in the Chinese Civil War.

ROC Republic of China, Taiwan's formal name, founded by the KMT in China and moved to Taiwan after the Chinese Civil War.

ROC presidents Chiang Kai-shek, 1948–75; Yen, Chia-kan (C. K. Yen), 1975–78; Chiang Ching-kuo, 1978–88; Lee Teng-hui, 1988–96 (unelected); 1996–2000 (elected by popular vote); Chen Shui-bian, 2000–08; Ma Ying-jeou, 2008–16; Tsai Ing-wen, 2016–24

Six Assurances These six semi-formal guidelines to US–Taiwan relations were established in 1982 as the US–China relationship was growing and the US–Taiwan relationship was changing. The intention of the assurances was to inform both Taiwan and China that the US would continue to support Taiwan regardless of how US–China relations developed.

strategic ambiguity The United States' dual deterrence strategy, it posits under which conditions it would support Taiwan in the event of a conflict. If the PRC attacks unprovoked, the US is more likely to defend Taiwan. If Taiwan declares formal de jure independence unilaterally, the US is less likely to defend Taiwan.

Sunflower Movement The 2014 protest sparked by the controversial Cross-Strait Service Trade Agreement. The protests began on 18 March and ended on 10 April. Activists began the protests in opposition to the bill, the KMT, and the direction of Cross-Strait relations, which many participants feared was on route to corrode Taiwan's democratic system. After a three-week long occupation of Taiwan's Legislative Yuan, activists successfully convinced the government to withdraw the bill. The protest was a watershed moment for Taiwanese politics, and launched a new wave of activists-turned-politicians and new political parties.

Tangwai The term given to opposition activists during the authoritarian era. *Tangwai*, meaning literally "outside the party", were loosely organized and promoted disparate causes, but were united in their opposition to the ruling KMT. They were instrumental in pressing for democratization from below and were the de facto forerunner of Taiwan's first opposition party, the DPP.

Three Communiqués These three joint statements between the United States and the PRC over ten years are part of the foundations of US–China relations. They also establish how each country views Taiwan and how the other will approach their own relationship to Taiwan. The first established the new relationship between the US and the PRC. The second formally saw the US switch recognition from the ROC to the PRC. The third expresses both sides intentions to grow relations while also further establishing each other's attitudes towards Taiwan.

TPP The Taiwan People's Party, founded by former Taipei mayor Ko Wen-je, this party tries to present itself as a middle choice within Taiwanese politics, but tends to lean more towards friendly relations with China like the KMT.

Waishengren Han Chinese who fled to Taiwan after the KMT lost the civil war.

Guide to further reading

We can attest from long experience that the best way to nurture a sense of connection is to visit Taiwan, which we strongly recommend. Taiwan also produces a wealth of film, music, literature and pop cultural content to explore, much of it available online. However, befitting our role as academics, we finish here by recommending some of our favourite readings for deepening knowledge on various aspects of Taiwan (listed in alphabetical order). The field of Taiwan Studies is thriving and this selection represents the mere tip of the iceberg.

ACADEMIC SOURCES

Christopher Achen & T.-Y. Wang's *The Taiwan Voter* (Ann Arbor, MI: University of Michigan Press, 2017) is an edited collection of studies by Taiwanese political scientists and is a go-to for those who want to better understand the nuts and bolts of electoral politics in Taiwan. Topics in this volume cover how we know China is the paramount issue in electoral politics, how Taiwan ended up becoming polarized along blue-green lines, and the relationships between voters and parties. Despite the political science orientation of the volume, the writing of these essays are both accessible and valuable for anyone interested in Taiwanese politics.

Melissa Brown's *Is Taiwan Chinese? The Impact of Culture, Power and Migration on Changing Identities* (Berkeley, CA: University of California Press, 2004), with its "controversial" title, is a masterful study based on meticulous ethnographic case studies and historical data analysis. It establishes the fluidity of identity in Taiwanese and to lesser extent

Chinese contexts, and a challenge to arguments that identity has fixed characteristics that are immune to political malleability. Its focus is on the place of Taiwan's Indigenous peoples and the competing constructions and impositions of their identity through Taiwan's various experiences with colonialism.

Allen Chun's *Forget Chineseness: On the Geopolitics of Cultural Identification* (Albany, NY: SUNY Press, 2017) is a deeply thought-provoking study of identity formation and a must-read for those wanting to understand more how Chinese identity forms and varies across the Asia Pacific. Chun looks at Taiwan, Hong Kong, Singapore, and China, and how their historical contexts have produced vastly different relationships with China and Chinese identity. Despite the provocative title, this book is not actually about forgetting Chineseness, but reimagining how we approach cultural and national identity in relation to China.

Dafydd Fell's *Government and Politics in Taiwan* (Abingdon: Routledge, 2018) is an accessible and comprehensive introductory text which covers all of the salient dimensions of Taiwanese politics including the transition to democracy, party and electoral politics and cross-Strait relations. It supplies the amount of detail and nuance, but it does so with great clarity, engaging case studies and some charming personal reflections on the author's own experiences as a student and academic in Taiwan over three decades. It is an indispensable text for getting a handle on Taiwanese politics.

Ming-sho Ho's *Challenging Beijing's Mandate of Heaven: Taiwan's Sunflower Movement and Hong Kong's Umbrella Movement* (Philadelphia, PA: Temple University Press, 2019) shows protest as a central feature of Taiwanese contemporary politics. But perhaps no protest has influenced today's political context more than the 2014 Sunflower Movement. Ho explores not just this watershed moment in Taiwanese history, but also how it relates to Hong Kong's Umbrella Movement, an equally era-defining protest. This study is not only useful for those interested in Taiwanese protest, but also how protest and resistance to Chinese coercion brings different parts of East Asian civil society together.

Syaru Shirley Lin's *Taiwan's China Dilemma: Contested Identities and Multiple Interests in Taiwan's Cross-Strait Economic Policy* (Redwood City, CA: Stanford University Press, 2016) presents how Taiwan's national identity has played a role in the economic development of

relations between the ROC and PRC. Lin shows how these two economies have developed and become increasingly integrated over time.
She also explains how different Taiwanese presidents' economic policies
towards the PRC have varied over time. This book offers an important
exploration in how identity and economics have played a central role in
Cross-Strait relations.

Mikael Mattlin's *Politicized Society: The Long Shadow of Taiwan's
One-Party Legacy* (Copenhagen: NIAS Press, 2011) shows the KMT
was able to survive and indeed flourish post-democratization because
it strategically determined the parameters of liberalization, choosing
what to change and modifying its behaviour accordingly. Without a
complete break from the ancien regime, the KMT was able to shape
post-democratic political and social structures and continue to benefit from them. More than a decade removed from publication, some
incomplete reforms have been addressed, but not entirely, and this book
is essential reading on the long legacy of KMT authoritarianism.

Shelley Rigger's *From Opposition to Power: Taiwan's Democratic Progressive Party* (Boulder, CO: Lynne Rienner, 2001) is a fundamental study
of the evolution and emergence of the DPP as the major opposition party
to the KMT. The story of the *tangwai* opposition movement and how
activists resisted KMT authoritarianism to press for reforms is expertly
and thrillingly told. It is an indispensable guide to how the DPP became
the force it is in contemporary Taiwanese politics and full of inspiring
accounts from the struggle for democratization. It is a reminder that the
precious freedoms that Taiwanese people enjoy today were the result of
a long and arduous fight.

Dominic Meng-Hsuan Yang's *The Great Exodus from China: Trauma,
Memory and Identity in Modern Taiwan* (Cambridge: Cambridge
University Press, 2020) tells a deeply empathetic and moving history of
waishengren refugees who fled to Taiwan with the KMT. Yang explores
the construction of *waishengren* identity and the challenges this group
of Chinese refugees faced despite their privileged position within
Taiwanese society. Yang ends by opening up about his own family's history as *benshengren* who suffered greatly under the KMT's authoritarian rule, but how through his research he found a new level of empathy
and compassion for the *waishengren* experience, or as he describes,
"The pain of displaced people who displaced people" (Yang: 259). This

wonderful work of history is a must-read for those who want to begin to understand the complexities of not just the generational *waishengren* and *benshengren* divide, but how important historical memory and memory narratives shape contemporary politics.

U.S.–Taiwan Relations: Will China's Challenge Lead to a Crisis? by Ryan Hass, Bonnie Glaser and Richard Bush is the latest and most comprehensive book introducing US–Taiwan relations. As the foremost experts on Taiwan's foreign policy in Washington, DC, these three authors have collaborated to create an incredibly informative guide on US–Taiwan. It is not only a historical exploration of the US–Taiwan relationship but also provides insights into its future trajectory. It delves deep into the guiding policies and communiques that shape both the US–Taiwan and US–China relationships, illustrating their continued relevance in maintaining peace today. For individuals interested in US foreign policy towards Taiwan and China, this book is an indispensable resource.

NON-ACADEMIC SOURCES

Green Island: A Novel by Shawna Yang Ryan (New York: Penguin, 2016) is a brilliant work of historical fiction that tells the story of the Tsai family, a *benshengren* family living in Taiwan. Beginning with the 228 incident, the family patron Dr Tsai is taken prisoner during the White Terror and is eventually freed and returns to his family. The story explores the life of a family that lives through martial law, migration to the United States, and eventual democratization in Taiwan.

Made in Taiwan: Recipes and Stories from the Island Nation by Clarissa Wei (New York: Simon & Schuster, 2023) is the premier cookbook on Taiwanese cuisine. This volume not only includes recipes, but also detailed histories and backgrounds of where some of Taiwan's most famous dishes come from. The politics of Taiwan and China are not lost in these recipes either; Wei makes a particular effort to include how Taiwan's political contestation has impacted its cuisine over time in her writing.

City of Sadness (3-H Films, 1989) is one of Taiwanese director Hou Hsiao-hsien's masterpieces. The film follows the lives of a Taiwanese family during the transition between the Japanese colonial period and the KMT martial law era. It was one of the first Taiwanese films to openly depict the 228 incident and remains an important piece of Taiwanese cinematic history.

On Happiness Road (Happiness Road Productions, 2017) is a Taiwanese animated film directed by Sung Hsin-yin, which made a huge splash around the animation world from Japan to the United States. The film follows the life of a small Taiwanese girl born in Taipei and the world she grew up in from martial law through democratization. The visuals are stunning and it presents one of the most creative and imaginative ways of learning about Taiwanese history.

Ghost Island Media (https://ghostisland.media/en/) is a native Taiwan podcast company that has become one of the most valuable resources for audio content on Taiwan. They have a wide variety of English and Mandarin language programmes that range from learning about gender equality, environmental activism, and contemporary Taiwanese politics.

The video game-turned-Netflix series, *Detention* (2017/2020) tells the story of high school students trapped in their school during Taiwan's White Terror. While not for the faint of heart, *Detention* offers a unique way to experience one of Taiwan's darkest and most complex moments of history through two alternative mediums.

ENGLISH-LANGUAGE OUTLETS ON TAIWAN POLITICS

The Reporter (https://www.twreporter.org/a/about-us-english-version) is one of Taiwan's premier long-form news outlets that thoughtfully cover stories in-depth. *Taiwan Insight* (https://taiwaninsight.org/) is the Taiwan Studies magazine based at the University of Nottingham and which publishes a wide variety of Taiwan related content. Frozen Garlic (https://frozengarlic.wordpress.com/) run by political scientist Nathan Batto, is one of the best English-language blogs about Taiwanese elections. *New Bloom* (https://newbloommag.net/) is an online English-language magazine that covers Taiwanese politics with a focus on activism and youth politics. *Taiwan Gazette* (https://www.taiwangazette.org/) provides translations of news and reports out of Taiwan to help share stories to the English-speaking world.

References

ABC News 2021. "Full transcript of ABC News' George Stephanopoulos' interview with President Joe Biden". 19 August. https://abcnews.go.com/Politics/full-transcript-abc-news-george-stephanopoulos-interview-president/story?id=79535643.

Achen, C. & T.-Y. Wang 2017. *The Taiwan Voter*. Ann Arbor, MI: University of Michigan Press.

Ahn, J.-H. & T. Lin 2019. "The politics of apology: the 'Tzuyu Scandal' and transnational dynamics of K-Pop". *International Communication Gazette* 81(2): 158–75.

Bing, N. 2017. "Taiwan's Go South Policy: déjà vu all over again?" *Contemporary Southeast Asia* 39(1): 96–126.

Bosco, J. 1992. "Taiwan factions: *guanxi*, patronage and the state in local politics". *Ethnology* 31(2): 157–93.

Brown, K. 2020. "The Beijing perspective: the political and diplomatic context for Taiwan and the World Health Assembly". *International Journal of Taiwan Studies* 3(1): 28–43.

Brown, M. 2004. *Is Taiwan Chinese? The Impact of Culture, Power, and Migration on Changing Identities*. Berkeley, CA: University of California Press.

Buckley, C. & A. Wang 2016. "Singer's apology for waving Taiwan flag stirs backlash of its own". *New York Times*, 13 January. https://www.nytimes.com/2016/01/17/world/asia/taiwan-china-singer-chou-tzu-yu.html.

Bush, R. 2017. "A One-China policy primer". Brookings East Asia Policy Paper 10: 1–30. https://www.brookings.edu/wp-content/uploads/2017/03/one-china-policy-primer-web-final.pdf.

Bush, R. 2021. *Difficult Choices: Taiwan's Quest for Security and the Good Life*. Washington, DC: Brookings Institution Press.

Campbell, C. 2021. "Inside the Taiwan firm that makes the world's tech run". *Time*, 1 October. https://time.com/6102879/semiconductor-chip-shortage-tsmc/.

Chan, N., L. Nachman & C. Mok 2021. "TRENDS: a red flag for participation: the influence of Chinese mainlandization on political behavior in Hong Kong". *Political Research Quarterly* 74(1): 3–17.

Chang, H.-C. & R. Holt 2007. "Symbols in conflict: *Taiwan* (Taiwan) and *Zhongguo* (China) in Taiwan's identity politics". *Nationalism and Ethnic Politics* 13(1): 129–65.

Chen, C.-J. & V. Zheng 2022. "Changing attitudes toward China in Taiwan and Hong Kong in the Xi Jinping era". *Journal of Contemporary China* 31(134): 250–66.

Chen, Y.-J. 2022. "'One China' contention in China–Taiwan relations: law, politics and identity". *China Quarterly* 252: 1025–44.

Cheng, E. 2022. "Taiwan's trade with China is far bigger than its trade with the US". CNBC, 14 August. https://www.cnbc.com/2022/08/05/taiwans-trade-with-china-is-far-bigger-than-its-trade-with-the-us.html.

Cheng, M. 2022. "Low pay drives 40% of 'Gold Card' expats to leave Taiwan". *Commonwealth Magazine*, 12 December. https://english.cw.com.tw/article/article.action?id=3357.

Cheng, T. 1989. "Democratizing the quasi-leninist regime in Taiwan". *World Politics* 41(4): 471–99.

Cheng, T. & L. Li 2022. "Apple warns suppliers to follow China rules on 'Taiwan' labelling". Nikkei, 5 August. https://asia.nikkei.com/Spotlight/Supply-Chain/Apple-warns-suppliers-to-follow-China-rules-on-Taiwan-labeling.

Chin, K. 2003. *Heijin: Organized Crime, Business, and Politics in Taiwan*. Armonk, NJ: M. E. Sharpe.

Ching, L. 2000. "Savage construction and civility making: the Musha Incident and aboriginal representations in colonial Taiwan". *Positions: East Asia Cultures Critique* 8(3): 795–818.

Ching, L. 2001. *Becoming Japanese: Colonial Taiwan and the Politics of Identity Formation*. Berkeley, CA: University of California Press.

Chiou, C. 1986. "Politics of alienation and polarization: Taiwan's Tangwai in the 1980s". *Bulletin of Concerned Asian Scholars* 18(3): 16–28.

Chou, Y. & A. Nathan 1987. "Democratizing transition in Taiwan". *Asian Survey* 27(3): 277–99.

Christensen, T. *et al.* 2022. "How to avoid a war over Taiwan: threats, assurances, and effective deterrence". *Foreign Affairs*, 13 October. https://ssp.mit.edu/publications/2022/how-to-avoid-a-war-over-taiwan-threats-assurances-and-effective-deterrence.

Chu, J.-J. 2000. "Nationalism and self-determination: the identity politics in Taiwan". *Journal of Asian and African Studies* 35(3): 303–21.

Chu, R.-X. & C.-T. Huang 2021. "The day after the apology: a critical discourse analysis of President Tsai's national apology to Taiwan's indigenous peoples". *Discourse Studies* 23(1): 84–101.

Chu, Y. 2004. "Taiwan's national identity politics and the prospect of cross-strait relations". *Asian Survey* 44(4): 484–512.

Chun, A. 1994. "From nationalism to nationalizing: cultural imagination and state formation in postwar Taiwan". *Australian Journal of Chinese Affairs* 31: 49–69.

Chun, A. 2017. *Forget Chineseness: On the Geopolitics of Cultural Identification.* Albany, NY: SUNY Press.

Demirjian, K. 2022. "Pentagon warns of China's plans for dominance in Taiwan and beyond". *Washington Post*, 22 November. https://www.washingtonpost.com/national-security/2022/11/29/pentagon-china-military-report-taiwan/.

DPP 1999. "Resolution on Taiwan's Future". 8 May. https://www.taiwandc.org/nws-9920.htm.

Drun, J. 2017. "One China, multiple interpretations". Center for Advanced China Research, 28 December.

Drun, J. 2021. "Status quo? What status quo?" *Journal of Indo-Pacific Affairs*, March.

Economist, The 2021. "The most dangerous place on Earth". *The Economist*, 1 May. https://www.economist.com/weeklyedition/2021-05-01.

Edmondson, R. 2002. "The February 28 incident and national identity". In S. Corcuff (ed.), *Memories of the Future: National Identity Issues and the Search for a New Taiwan*, 25–46. Armonk, NJ: M. E. Sharpe.

Ellis, S. & A. Chang 2021. "Tycoon targeted by China speaks out against Taiwan independence". Bloomberg, 30 November. https://www.bloomberg.com/news/articles/2021-11-30/tycoon-targeted-by-china-speaks-out-against-taiwan-independence?leadSource=uverify%20wall.

Fell, D. 2005. "Measuring and explaining party change in Taiwan: 1991–2004". *Journal of East Asian Studies* 5(1): 105–33.

Fell, D. 2006. *Party Politics in Taiwan: Party Change and the Democratic Evolution of Taiwan, 1991–2004.* Abingdon: Routledge.

Fell, D. 2018. *Government and Politics in Taiwan.* Abingdon: Routledge.

Focus Taiwan 2021. "Almost 90% of Taiwanese oppose 'one country two systems'". 9 September. https://www.cna.com.tw/amp/news/acn/202109090297.aspx.

Focus Taiwan 2022. "American observers weigh pros and cons of Pelosi visit to Taiwan". 3 August. https://focustaiwan.tw/politics/202208030015.

Foreign Affairs 2022. "Should the United States pledge to defend Taiwan?

Foreign Affairs asks the experts". *Foreign Affairs*, 15 November. https://www.foreignaffairs.com/ask-the-experts/should-united-states-pledge-defend-taiwan.

Fulco, M. 2022. "Is the Taiwan Policy Act good for Taipei?" *Japan Times*, 30 October. https://www.japantimes.co.jp/news/2022/10/30/asia-pacific/taiwan-policy-act/.

Garver, J. 2015. *China's Quest: The History of the Foreign Relations of the People's Republic of China*. Oxford: Oxford University Press.

Glaser, B., S. Kennedy & D. Mitchell 2018. *The New Southbound Policy: Deepening Taiwan's Regional Integration*. Lexington, KY: Rowman & Littlefield.

Glaser, B. *et al.* 2020. "Dire straits: should American support for Taiwan be ambiguous?" *Foreign Affairs*, 24 September. https://www.foreignaffairs.com/articles/united-states/2020-09-24/dire-straits.

Harold, S., N. Beauchamp-Mustafaga & J. Hornung 2021. *Chinese Disinformation Efforts on Social Media*. Santa Monica, CA: Rand.

Hass, R., B. Glaser & R. Bush 2023. *US–Taiwan Relations: Will China's Challenge Lead to a Crisis?* Washington, DC: Brookings Institution Press.

Hayton, B. 2020. *The Invention of China*. New Haven, CT: Yale University Press.

Heé, N. 2014. "Taiwan under Japanese rule: showpiece of a model colony? Historiographical tendencies in narrating colonialism". *History Compass* 12(8): 632–41.

Hioe, B. 2022. "China slaps export bans on Taiwanese goods – again". *The Diplomat*, 16 December. https://thediplomat.com/2022/12/china-slaps-export-bans-on-taiwanese-goods-again/.

Ho, M. 2015. "Occupy congress in Taiwan: political opportunity, threat, and the Sunflower Movement". *Journal of East Asian Studies* 15(1): 69–97.

Ho, M. 2019. *Challenging Beijing's Mandate of Heaven: Taiwan's Sunflower Movement and Hong Kong's Umbrella Movement*. Philadelphia, PA: Temple University Press.

Ho, S. 1987. "Economics, economic bureaucracy, and Taiwan's economic development". *Pacific Affairs* 60(2): 226–47.

Holbig, H. 2020. "Be water, my friend: Hong Kong's 2019 anti-extradition protests". *International Journal of Sociology* 50(4): 325–37.

Hsiau, A. 2003. *Contemporary Taiwanese Cultural Nationalism*. Abingdon: Routledge.

Hsieh, J. 2017. "The changing identities of Taiwan's plains indigenous peoples". In B. Jacobs & P. Kang (eds), *Changing Taiwanese Identities*, 12–26. Abingdon: Routledge.

Hsieh, J. & E. Niou 2005. "Measuring Taiwanese public opinion on Taiwanese independence". *China Quarterly* 181: 158–68.

Huang, C. 2005. "Dimensions of Taiwanese/Chinese identity and national identity in Taiwan: a latent class analysis". *Journal of Asian and African Studies* 40(1/2): 51–70.

Hughes, C. 1997. *Taiwan and Chinese Nationalism: National Identity and Status in International Society*. Abingdon: Routledge.

Ihara, K. 2019. "Chinese tourists to Taiwan plunge 60% in September". Nikkei, 28 October. https://asia.nikkei.com/Politics/International-relations/ Chinese-tourists-to-Taiwan-plunge-60-in-September.

Jacobs, J. 2012. *Democratizing Taiwan*. Amsterdam: Brill.

Ji, Y. 2006. "China's anti-secession law and the risk of war in the Taiwan Strait". *Contemporary Security Policy* 27(2): 237–57.

Ko, A. *et al.* 2014. "Early Austronesians: into and out of Taiwan". *American Journal of Human Genetics* 94(3): 426–36.

Ko, S. 2021. "Pineapple diplomacy? China's Taiwan import ban prompts sales surge in Japan". *Japan Times*, 15 March. https://www.japantimes.co.jp/news/ 2021/03/15/business/pineapples-china-taiwan-imports-japan/.

Keng, S. & G. Schubert 2010. "Agents of Taiwan–China unification? The political roles of Taiwanese business people in the process of cross-Strait integration". *Asian Survey* 50(2): 287–310.

Kim, J. 2019. "Star Wars: how Taiwan's celebrities became pawns in the cross-Strait struggle". *The Diplomat*, 26 December. https://thediplomat.com/2019/ 12/star-wars-how-taiwans-celebrities-became-pawns-in-the-cross-strait-struggle/.

Lamley, H. 1968. "The 1895 Taiwan republic: a significant episode in modern Chinese history". *Journal of Asian Studies* 27(4): 739–62.

Lau, S. & R. Momtaz 2021. "China downgrades Lithuania's diplomatic status over Taiwan row". Politico, 21 November. https://www.politico.eu/article/ china-downgrades-diplomatic-relations-with-lithuania-over-taiwan-representative-office/.

Lawrence, S. 2020. "President Reagan's six assurances to Taiwan". Congressional Research Service. https://sgp.fas.org/crs/row/IF11665.pdf.

Lee, Y. 2021. "2 charts show how much the world depends on Taiwan for semiconductors". CNBC, 15 March. https://www.cnbc.com/2021/03/16/2-charts-show-how-much-the-world-depends-on-taiwan-for-semi conductors.html.

Li, Y., P. James & A. Drury 2009. "Diversionary dragons, or 'talking tough in Taipei': cross-Strait relations in the new millennium". *Journal of East Asian Studies* 9(3): 369–98.

Lieberthal, K. 2005. "Preventing a war over Taiwan". *Foreign Affairs* 84: 53–63.

Liff, A. 2022. "Japan, Taiwan and the "One China" framework after 50 years".

China Quarterly 252: 1066–93.

Lin, J. 2022. "Nostalgia for Japanese colonialism: historical memory and postcolonialism in Contemporary Taiwan". *History Compass* 20(11): doi:10.1111/hic3.12751.

Lin, S. 2016. *Taiwan's China Dilemma: Contested Identities and Multiple Interests in Taiwan's Cross-Strait Economic Policy.* Redwood City, CA: Stanford University Press.

Liu, Z. 2022. "Mainland suspends export of natural sand to Taiwan". *China Daily*, 3 August. https://www.chinadaily.com.cn/a/202208/03/WS62e9da 7ea310fd2b29e70020.html.

Mattlin, M. 2004. "Referendum as a form of Zaoshi: the instrumental domestic political functions of Taiwan's referendum ploy". *Issues and Studies* 40(2): 155–85.

Mattlin, M. 2011. *Politicized Society: The Long Shadow of Taiwan's One-Party Legacy.* Copenhagen: NiAS Press.

Miller, C. 2022. *Chip War: The Fight for the World's Most Critical Technology.* New York: Simon & Schuster.

Nachman, L. 2018. "Misalignment between social movements and political parties in Taiwan's 2016 election: not all grass roots are green". *Asian Survey* 58(5): 874–97.

Nachman, L. 2020. "From sunflowers to suits: how spatial openings affect movement party formation". In T. Gold & S. Veg (eds), *Sunflowers and Umbrellas: Social Movements, Expressive Practices, and Political Culture in Taiwan and Hong Kong*, 200–27. Berkeley, CA: University of California Press.

Nachman, L. & B. Hioe 2019. "Friends from Hong Kong: Taiwan's refugee problem". *The Diplomat*, 23 October.

Nachman, L., N. Chan & J. Mok 2020. "Hong-Kongers say Taiwan is their first choice as exile looms". *Foreign Policy*, 8 July.

Nachman, L., N. Chan & J. Mok 2021. "Taiwanese are sympathetic but uncertain about Hong Kong refugees". *Foreign Policy*, 5 August.

Newland, S. 2022. "Paradiplomacy as a response to international isolation: the case of Taiwan". *Pacific Review.* doi:10.1080/09512748.2022.2025889.

Ngerng, R. 2022. "Taiwan's minimum wage is one of the lowest in its league". *The News Lens*, 9 February. https://international.thenewslens.com/feature/roy-ngerng-minimum-wage/162570.

Olcott, E. 2021. "Taiwan seizes chance to host foreign reporters kicked out of China". *Financial Times*, 21 April. https://www.ft.com/content/ab588fed-fc21-4b19-b601-538d87d79db3.

Pan, J. 2021. "Groups rally for jailed Lee Ming-che". *Taipei Times*, 31 August.

https://www.taipeitimes.com/News/taiwan/archives/2021/08/31/2003763533.

Papada, E. *et al.* 2023. *Defiance in the Face of Autocratization: Democracy Report 2023.* University of Gothenburg, Varieties of Democracy Institute (V-Dem Institute).

Radio Taiwan International 2022. "Philippines has plans to evacuate nationals from Taiwan in the event of a war". 12 August. https://en.rti.org.tw/news/view/id/2008037.

Rawnsley, G. & M.-Y. Rawnsley 2004. "Media reform since 1989". *China Perspectives* 56: 46–55.

Rawnsley, M.-Y. & C. Feng 2014. "Anti-media monopoly policies and further democratisation in Taiwan". *Journal of Current Chinese Affairs* 43(3): 105–28.

Rawnsley, M.-Y., J. Smyth & J. Sullivan 2016. "Taiwanese media reform". *Journal of the British Association for Chinese Studies* 6(6): 66–80.

Rich, T. & A. Dahmer 2020. "Taiwanese public perceptions of diplomatic recognition: an experimental analysis". *International Journal of Taiwan Studies* 3(2): 247–67.

Rich, T. & A. Dahmer 2022. "Should I stay or should I go? Diplomatic recognition of Taiwan, 1950–2016". *International Journal of Taiwan Studies* 5(2): 353–74.

Rich, T. & J. Sullivan 2016. "Elections". In G. Schubert (ed.), *Routledge Handbook of Contemporary Taiwan*, 119–36. Abingdon: Routledge.

Rigger, S. 1994. "Machine Politics in the New Taiwan: Institutional Reform and Electoral Strategy in the Republic of China on Taiwan". Dissertation, Harvard University.

Rigger, S. 2001a. *From Opposition to Power: Taiwan's Democratic Progressive Party*. Boulder, CO: Lynne Rienner.

Rigger, S. 2001b. "Regional perspectives and domestic imperatives: maintaining the status quo: what it means, and why the Taiwanese prefer it". *Cambridge Review of International Affairs* 14(2): 103–14.

Rigger, S. 2002. *Politics in Taiwan: Voting for Reform*. New York: Routledge.

Rigger, S. 2011 *Why Taiwan Matters: Small Island, Global Powerhouse*. Lanham, MD: Rowman & Littlefield.

Rigger, S. 2021. *The Tiger Leading the Dragon: How Taiwan Propelled China's Economic Rise*. Lanham, MD: Rowman & Littlefield.

Rigger, S. *et al.* 2022. "Why is unification so unpopular in Taiwan? It's the PRC political system, not just culture". Brookings blog, 7 February. https://www.brookings.edu/blog/order-from-chaos/2022/02/07/why-is-unification-so-unpopular-in-taiwan-its-the-prc-political-system-not-just-culture/.

Riker, W. 1982. "The two-party system and Duverger's law: an essay on the history of political science". *American Political Science Review* 76(4): 753–66.

Ross, R. 1997. *Negotiating Cooperation: The United States and China, 1969–1989*. Redwood City, CA: Stanford University Press.

Ross, R. 2002. "Navigating the Taiwan Strait: deterrence, escalation dominance, and US–China relations". *International Security* 27(2): 48–85.

Ross, R. 2006. "Explaining Taiwan's revisionist diplomacy". *Journal of Contemporary China* 15(48): 443–58.

Rowen, I. 2015. "Inside Taiwan's sunflower movement: twenty-four days in a student-occupied parliament, and the future of the region". *Journal of Asian Studies* 74(1): 5–21.

Roy, D. 2003. *Taiwan: A Political History*. Ithaca, NY: Cornell University Press.

Schiffrin, H. 1970. *Sun Yat-sen and the Origins of the Chinese Revolution*. Berkeley, CA: University of California Press.

Schubert, G. 2004. "Taiwan's political parties and national identity: the rise of an overarching consensus". *Asian Survey* 44(4): 534–54.

Schubert, G. (ed). 2016. *Routledge Handbook of Contemporary Taiwan*. Abingdon: Routledge.

Scobell, A. 2000. "Show of force: Chinese soldiers, statesmen, and the 1995–1996 Taiwan Strait Crisis". *Political Science Quarterly* 115(2): 227–46.

Shattuck, T. 2020. "The race to zero? China's poaching of Taiwan's diplomatic allies". *Orbis* 64(2): 334–52.

Shen, J. 1999. "Sovereignty, statehood, self-determination, and the issue of Taiwan". *American University of International Law Review* 15: 1101–62.

Sheng, W. 2021. "China spends more importing semiconductors than oil". *Technode*, 29 April.

Shih, C. & M. Chen 2010. "Taiwanese identity and the memories of 2–28: a case for political reconciliation". *Asian Perspective* 34(4): 85–113.

Simon, S. 2010. "Negotiating power: elections and the constitution of indigenous Taiwan". *American Ethnologist* 37(4): 726–40.

Smith, C. 2008. "Taiwan's 228 incident and the politics of placing blame". *Past Imperfect* 14. doi:10.21971/P7XK5F.

Sullivan, J. 2008. "Campaign advertising and democracy in Taiwan". *China Quarterly* 196: 900–11.

Sullivan, J. & D. Lee 2018. "Soft power runs into popular geopolitics: western media frames democratic Taiwan". *International Journal of Taiwan Studies* 1(2): 273–300.

Sullivan, J. & W. Lowe 2010. "Chen Shui-bian: on independence". *China Quarterly* 203: 619–38.

Templeman, K. 2018. "When do electoral quotas advance indigenous representation? Evidence from the Taiwanese legislature". *Ethnopolitics* 17(5): 461–84.

Templeman, K. 2020. "How Taiwan stands up to China". *Journal of Democracy* 31(3): 85–99.

Templeman, K. 2022. "Taiwan is not Ukraine: stop linking their fates together". War on the Rocks, 27 January. https://warontherocks.com/2022/01/taiwan-is-not-ukraine-stop-linking-their-fates-together/.

Teng, E. 2004. *Taiwan's Imagined Geography: Chinese Colonial Travel Writing and Pictures, 1683–1895*. Cambridge, MA: Harvard University Asia Center.

Tian, Y. & B. Blanchard 2022. "China sanctions seven Taiwanese 'independence diehard' officials". Reuters, 16 August. https://www.reuters.com/world/china/china-sanctions-seven-taiwanese-officials-supporting-taiwan-independence-xinhua-2022-08-16/.

Tien, H. & Y. Chu 1996. "Building democracy in Taiwan". *China Quarterly* 148: 1141–70.

Tsai, T. & B. Cheng 2006. *The Silicon Dragon: High-Tech Industry in Taiwan*. Cheltenham: Elgar.

Tsang, S. 2006. *If China Attacks Taiwan*. New York: Routledge.

Tsang, S. (ed). 2008. *Taiwan and the International Community*. Bern: Peter Lang.

Tso, F.-N. 2020. "So close yet so far: the immigrant experience of Hong Kongers in Taiwan". *The Reporter*, 15 October.

Tsurumi, E. 1977. *Japanese Colonial Education in Taiwan, 1895–1945*. Cambridge, MA: Harvard University Press.

Tucker, N. (ed.) 2005. *Dangerous Strait: The US–Taiwan–China Crisis*. New York: Columbia University Press.

Tucker, N. & B. Glaser 2011. "Should the United States abandon Taiwan?" *Washington Quarterly* 34(4): 23–37.

US Trade Representative, Office of 2022. "U.S.–Taiwan trade facts". https://ustr.gov/countries-regions/china/taiwan.

Victor, D. 2021. "John Cena apologizes to China for calling Taiwan a country". *New York Times*, 5 May. https://www.nytimes.com/2021/05/25/world/asia/john-cena-taiwan-apology.html.

Wachman, A. 1994. *Taiwan: National Identity and Democratization*. Armonk, NJ: M. E. Sharpe.

Wang, Z. 2008. "National Humiliation, history education, and the politics of historical memory: patriotic education campaign in China". *International Studies Quarterly* 52(4): 783–806.

Ward, A. & Q. Forgey 2022. "Biden Beetlejuiced the end of Taiwan strategic ambiguity". Politico, 23 May. https://www.politico.com/newsletters/national-security-daily/2022/05/23/biden-beetlejuiced-the-end-of-strategic-ambiguity-toward-taiwan-00034459.

Wee, S.-L. 2018. "Giving in to China, U.S. airlines drop Taiwan (in name at least)". *New York Times*, 25 July. https://www.nytimes.com/2018/07/25/business/taiwan-american-airlines-china.html.

White House 2021. "Remarks by President Biden in a CNN Town Hall with Anderson Cooper". 21 October. https://www.whitehouse.gov/briefing-room/speeches-remarks/2021/10/22/remarks-by-president-biden-in-a-cnn-town-hall-with-anderson-cooper-2/.

Winkler, S. 2014. "Taiwan in international organizations: new road ahead or dead-end?" In J.-P. Cabestan & J. DeLisle (eds), *Political Changes in Taiwan Under Ma Ying-jeou*, 265–82. New York: Routledge.

Wu, D. 2021. "China targets corporate backers of Taiwan's ruling party". Bloomberg, 22 November. https://www.bloomberg.com/news/articles/2021-11-22/china-sets-sights-on-corporate-backers-of-taiwan-s-independence?leadSource=uverify%20wall.

Wu, Y. 2000. "Theorizing on relations across the Taiwan Strait: nine contending approaches". *Journal of Contemporary China* 9(25): 407–28.

Wuthnow, J. & P. Saunders 2017. *Chinese Military Reform in the Age of Xi Jinping: Drivers, Challenges, and Implications*. Washington, DC: National Defense University Press.

Yang, D. 2020. *The Great Exodus from China: Trauma, Memory, and Identity in Modern Taiwan*. Cambridge: Cambridge University Press.

Yen, W.-T. 2020. "Taiwan's COVID-19 management: developmental state, digital governance, and state-society synergy". *Asian Politics & Policy* 12(3): 455–68.

Zhao, S. 2022. "Is Beijing's long game on Taiwan about to end? Peaceful unification, brinkmanship, and military takeover". *Journal of Contemporary China*. doi:10.1080/10670564.2022.2124349.

Zhong, Y. 2016. "Explaining national identity shift in Taiwan". *Journal of Contemporary China* 25(99): 336–52.

Zuo, X. 2021. "Unbalanced deterrence: coercive threat, reassurance and the US–China rivalry in Taiwan Strait". *Pacific Review* 34(4): 547–76.

Index